200 TIPS
for Growing

VEGETABLES

in the

PACIFIC NORTHWEST

Happy Gardening
Maggie Stuckey

Maggie Stuckey

CHICAGO
REVIEW
PRESS

Time spent working in your garden
will not be deducted from your life.

Library of Congress Cataloging-in-Publication Data

Stuckey, Maggie
  200 tips for growing vegetables in the Pacific Northwest / Maggie Stuckey. — 1st ed.
      p.   cm.
  Includes index.
  ISBN 1-55652-254-1 (paper : alk. paper)
  I. Vegetable gardening—Northwest, Pacific.
  I. Title.
SB321.5.N58S78   1996
635'.09795—dc20   95-43278
                                                          CIP

First Edition
Published by Chicago Review Press, Incorporated
814 North Franklin Street
Chicago, Illinois 60610

ISBN 1-55652-254-1

5 4 3 2 1

CONTENTS

❦ ❦ ❦

INTRODUCTION

❦ ❦ ❦

For all those who live in the Pacific Northwest and would like to grow your own vegetables, there is good news and bad news.

The good news is the weather.

The Pacific Northwest is blessed with many qualities and conditions that make it gardener's heaven. Even though we seem very far north, the winters are usually mild; the summers are pleasant but (usually) not scorching. The northerly latitude means we have long hours of sunlight in the summer months. We are blessed with many areas of wondrously fertile soil.

And, because agriculture is a significant industry in most of the region, we are within a turnip's throw of local growers, nurseries, and seed companies that specialize in plants that do well in this region. For home gardeners, this creates a wonderful side benefit: we are surrounded by an extraordinarily large number of very knowledgeable people.

I'm willing to bet that with just two phone calls you can find out anything you need to know: call any one friend who gardens and ask, "Who do you know that knows about parsnips [or raspberries, or powdery mildew, or whatever]?" Chances are your friend can refer you to the perfect person; at worst, that person will suggest someone else and you'll have to make a third call. Gardeners are generous folk by nature, and when you combine that with Northwestern friendliness, you'll realize you're in the perfect spot for creating a flourishing garden.

Now for the bad news—the weather.

The famous Northwest climate sometimes seems devilishly invented to wreak havoc on gardens. Rain and clay soils go together, and soil high in clay content compacts down to something as hard and heavy as concrete unless you take remedial action. The rain also is responsible for our acidic soils: terrific for rhododendrons, not so terrific for most vegetables.

The time when you most need to be outside doing the heavy work—early spring—is the time you least feel like venturing out into dreary weather. The overall dampness is the perfect medium for fungal diseases, and the many months of soggy soil and wet vegetation create the perfect breeding ground for the Garden Pest from Hell: slugs.

As soon as things start to dry out a bit, aphids appear. And morning glories. And wild blackberries. (And if you think those last two sound like good things to have in your garden, you've obviously just moved here.)

All these problems can, with work, be overcome. What you cannot improve by virtue of your own labor is the climate itself—the short growing season. The winter and spring months are mild compared to other parts of the country at similar latitudes, but we don't get consistently warm temperatures until June. Then often the cool weather moves in before the vegetable plants have really begun to produce in earnest. We call them "green tomato years"—the warm weather comes too late, or the cool weather too soon, for tomatoes (and other vegetables) to mature. So you have done all that work for nothing.

To get around this, gardeners learn to concentrate on varieties bred especially for our climate. We've also learned, by trial and error, lots of tricks for beating the odds. Sharing those tips is what this book is all about.

The information presented here came from many sources: Culture information provided in seed catalogs. Public appearances by local garden experts like Ed Hume and Vern Nelson. The teachings of Peter Chan, who introduced many Oregonians to the Chinese intensive raised-bed system 20 years ago and charmed us all with his gentle manner and generous spirit. And most especially Carolyn Clark, popular columnist and an enormously knowledgeable gardener, to whom I owe great thanks.

In the final analysis, we all got these ideas from the same place: the accumulated wisdom of generations of gardeners, who patiently took us by the hand and lovingly taught us what they knew. We can thank them by passing on new ideas we come up with. In the garden, as in life, we all are here to help each other.

STARTING FROM SCRATCH

❦ ❦ ❦

Where to Put the Garden

1 **Find the sunniest spot.** Vegetables need at least 6 hours of sunlight (rule of thumb). Put your vegetable garden in the part of your yard that gets the most sun. If you already have flowers planted in that spot, intermix the vegetables right along with them. Just be sure to think about the final size of the vegetable plant; wide-ranging zucchini vines are probably not a good idea. And who says vegetables have to be in the backyard? If your front yard gets the most sun, so be it.

2 **Find the place with the best soil.** The ideal soil for vegetable gardens is loose, fluffy in texture, a dark rich color, and very fertile. Unless the previous owner was a dedicated gardener, you probably don't have that kind of soil in your yard.

There is much you can do to improve the soil (see tips 44–48), but make it easy on yourself: start with the best you have. Avoid, if possible, areas that are very rocky, or where you know chemicals have been used. If you have an old brush pile, you're in luck; the area under it is probably rich in decomposed organic material. One quick guide: where do you have the healthiest weeds?

Good drainage is important, too. If you have two possible sites, dig a hole in both places and fill with water; pick the spot where the water drains out faster. However, if you have to choose between soil and sun, use the spot that gets the best sun. You can always improve soil quality, but you can't do much about the sunshine.

3 **Put the garden where you can see it from the house.** This is not so critical in a botanical sense, but very good for the soul. If the available sunshine and soil allow it, position your garden where it is visible from the part of the house you spend the most time in. Each time you catch sight of it, you will feel proud of your accomplishments. You can also more easily keep an eye out for two- or four-legged critters.

4 **Think about water supply and access.** If you have several options, put the vegetable garden close to a water supply. Dragging hoses around every day in hot summer is not much fun. Also, is there a driveway (either yours or a neighbor's) close by, for bringing in large bags of soil amendments, a rototiller, lumber, and so forth?

5 **Within the garden area, pay attention to microclimates.** Bright white walls reflect light. Dark walls and blacktop driveways absorb heat. If you can put your vegetables nearby, you can take advantage. Remember that cold air sinks. If your garden area is on a slope, plant cold-tolerant vegetables like cole crops and lettuce at the bottom and frost-sensitive things like peppers and squash at the top.

6 **You can grow vegetables even if you don't have a yard.** If your own yard is unsuitable for gardening, or if you don't have a yard, you can still enjoy fresh vegetables. Grow vegetables in containers or hanging baskets (see tips 177–181). Work out a deal with a neighbor, trading space for labor or half the produce.

Rent a plot in a community garden, if they're available in your area. If not, talk with local community groups, civic clubs, senior citizens' centers, any organization that has a building, about setting up a small garden area for the members; volunteer to help in exchange for some space for yourself.

What and When to Plant

7 **Match your choices to your growing conditions.** If all you have is a shady spot, don't even try to grow beans or squash; you'll just make yourself crazy. But you can have a world-class collection of lettuce and gourmet salad greens. Be realistic. Some things are just not meant to be. In high-elevation areas, your growing season may be only 80 days; don't waste your time with vegetables that take 110 days to mature.

8 **Grow what you like to eat.** It's easy to get carried away when reading a catalog or wandering the aisles of a large garden center. But stop and think: how much of this vegetable do you actually eat? If you usually cook winter squash only two or three times a year, do you really want to waste your garden space on it? On the other hand, if you enjoy canning you will want to plant large quantities of the vegetables everybody likes. The point is, give some thought to this; you don't have to grow everything.

⬦ **9** **Give the children one row of their own.** Plant things they like to eat or that are fun to grow. Help them choose things that are approximately appropriate, but as much as possible let them make the decisions and do the work.

Most kids will delight in growing baby carrots, and almost everyone likes to watch how fast radishes grow, even if they don't like to eat them. Children get a kick out of growing potatoes; they like digging them up. Pumpkins are fun, if your growing season is long enough; help children carve their names in the young fruit, and the carving stays as the pumpkins mature. Or if you have the space, let the children grow their own popcorn.

⬦ **10** **Choose varieties that do well in your area.** This will take a bit of research but it is well worth it. In fact, this is probably the single most important factor for success (except for soil quality, the other single most important). Buy seeds from companies who focus on short-season conditions (see Appendix). Read all catalogs carefully for maturity dates and other growing information.

Collect information everywhere you can, and keep notes. Walk around your neighborhood and talk to folks who are out working in their gardens; I've never met a gardener yet who wasn't willing to share. Read and clip newspaper articles by local writers. Attend shows, fairs, and special events sponsored by garden clubs and Master Gardeners. Call your local Extension Service office (see Appendix) with specific questions or to find out what publications they have available. Take classes from community colleges or adult education programs. Visit local nurseries that sell to walk-in customers and ask what they recommend. Talk to vendors at farmers' markets about varieties they've had good results with; if they have transplants for sale, you're in luck.

11 **Think in terms of plant families.** Groups of plants share important characteristics: ability to withstand cool weather, susceptibility to certain diseases, sunlight requirements, soil requirements, and so on. Many of your decisions are easier if you think of groups of cousins, rather than individual plants.

The main family groups are: Tomatoes, peppers, eggplant, and potatoes (solanums, aka nightshades); cucumbers, squash, pumpkins, and melons (cucurbits); beans and peas (legumes); cabbage, cauliflower, Brussels sprouts, kale, Chinese cabbage (brassicas, aka cole crops); onions, garlic, and shallots (alliums). The table greens—lettuce, Swiss chard, spinach—aren't a family in the strict sense but they need similar growing conditions. Botanically, the root crops belong to different families, but it's useful to think of them as a grouping too: beets, carrots, radishes, turnips, rutabagas.

Most of the time, whatever you learn about one member of a family applies to its cousins as well. Keep that in mind as you browse through this book; to save space, information appears in just one place, even though it may apply to several vegetables.

12 Don't rush things. Every February or March, we seem to get a week or so of luscious warm weather that makes every gardener's heart flutter. But be careful. If you have clay soil and you try to work it when it's wet, it turns to something akin to concrete. This is especially true if you rototill; you'll create a hardpan that you'll need a jackhammer to penetrate. And be leery of a hot spell in April and May; if you plant warm-season vegetables like tomatoes and squash, they're just going to sit there and pout until the soil and the air really warm up. You won't gain anything, and could possibly lose everything.

Rule of thumb: don't put summer vegetables in the ground until the lowest nighttime temperatures are consistently above 50°F.

13 **Plan a fall and winter garden.** In the low-elevation areas west of the Cascades, Mother Nature compensates for our late-arriving summer by letting us have relatively mild weather clear up through November. That kind of cool-but-not-freezing climate is perfect for lots of vegetables: all the greens, all the brassicas, and most of the root crops.

Sometimes this means you have to change your frame of mind, because for many of us "winter" and "gardening" don't belong in the same sentence. But if you take the time to learn which plants will survive a light frost, and which additional ones will carry through the winter with some mulch, you can have fresh vegetables almost all year round. And put the winter keepers in a separate spot. That way, you can till everything else in the fall without disturbing them.

WHAT ABOUT THE WEATHER?

❧ ❧ ❧

General Conditions and Regional Differences

14 **Elevation is as important as latitude.** I'll bet you know people back East who assume your hometown has bitterly cold weather because it's "so far north." My cousins in South Carolina don't believe their weather is colder than mine in Portland. How far north you are is broadly related to temperature, of course, but you have to go hundreds of miles (like from Grants Pass to Everett) before latitude makes a big difference. In contrast, change in elevation of one or two thousand feet can occur in under 20 miles, yet it makes an enormous difference in growing season.

High-elevation areas have very short growing seasons. If you live in the mountains in any of the Northwest states, or in one of the glorious high-desert regions, you have your work cut out for you. Up through June you'll have to try all the tricks to fool Mother Nature into thinking it's warmer than it is. Then in the summer you'll have to provide protection from the blazing sun during the day and still watch for frosty temperatures at night. You'll have to water all the time, and you'll probably have to add a lot of organic material to the dry, sandy soil. On the other hand, you *do* live in the mountains or the high desert.

◇15◇ **Day length is an important factor in how plants grow.** And that *is* related to latitude. The farther south you are, the shorter are summer days and longer are winter days. In September and October, there is more sunlight per day in northern California, giving gardeners there a longer season. Gardeners in Washington and northern Oregon need to remember that even though their fall temperatures are relatively mild, they have fewer hours of sunshine. So to say that the growing season is X number of days, based on temperatures alone, is deceiving.

16 **Strong persistent winds have an effect on garden conditions.** Not only do high winds tend to blow the plants to pieces, they also dry out the soil and lower the air temperature. In windy areas like the Columbia Gorge, you'll need to provide protection for the plants.

17 **All coastal areas have moderate temperatures year-round.** This is both good and bad. It seldom freezes at the coast and snow is so rare it makes the evening news, but the marine air with its high moisture content keeps temperatures a few degrees lower than inland areas all the time.

So plants are almost never killed by cold weather, and at the same time it isn't usually hot enough long enough for warm-season vegetables to thrive. Cool-season plants do very well: spinach, lettuce, all the cole crops, radishes, chard, things like that. Living at the beach has lots of wonderful benefits, but growing tomatoes is not one of them.

18 **The right time for putting things in the ground depends on your average frost dates.** A crucial piece of information for every gardener is the average frost dates in your area: the last day in spring and the first day in fall when you can expect temperatures below freezing. With some exceptions, vegetable plants are killed by a heavy freeze. Obviously these dates will vary from year to year; a good working average is all you need. All your planning is linked to this information: frost dates plus days to maturity.

The following dates reflect the average of weather data from 1950 to 1980. Use them as a general guide. Remember, though, that minor variations in topography can make a major difference in what you can successfully grow in your yard, and that there can be drastic swings from one year to the next. If you don't live close to one of these cities, ask your county Extension Office (see Appendix) for local dates.

Last Spring Frost	First Fall Frost
California	
*	*
Idaho, Boise	
May 8	October 9
Pocatello	
May 20	September 20
Montana, Missoula+	
May 25	September 10
Oregon, Eugene	
April 24	October 25

Pendleton
mid-April   late October

Portland
April 3   November 7

Washington, Seattle
March 24   November 11

Spokane
May 4   October 6

* In the Bay Area, killing frosts are rare. Inland, the climate is so varied it's difficult to give specific information here; readers should consult local nurseries or County Extension offices.

+ Dates for Missoula are approximate; specific data unavailable.

19 **Weather is fickle.** Even when you do everything right, if the weather turns nasty, you will probably lose some of your produce. Accept it: it will happen. It's not your fault.

Beating the Odds: Spring

20 **In very short season areas, try trench planting.** Where there is considerable variation between daytime and nighttime temperatures (as in the mountains or desert), trench planting may be your best bet.

It's rather like raised beds in reverse. Dig trenches 6 to 8 inches deep, piling up the soil into mounds between the trenches. Completely cover the mounds with clear plastic. Plant your vegetables in the trenches, then mulch heavily with straw, shredded leaves, or grass clippings.

To water, slide your hose under the mulch and flood the trench. The mulch holds the moisture in during the heat of the day, the plastic collects solar heat and keeps the soil from becoming too cold at night.

A variation on this technique for extremely cold areas: make the trench only about 4 inches deep and cover the entire bed loosely with clear plastic, including the trench. When the seedlings sprout and start pushing against the plastic, cut slits for them to grow through.

21 **Use a blanket of plastic to warm up the soil.** Two or three weeks before planting, spread the garden bed with plastic. Clear plastic, because it lets in all parts of the light spectrum, warms a few degrees more than black plastic, but promotes weed sprouting too. If you're putting out transplants of spring vegetables, you can leave the plastic in place; cut a slit or an X in the plastic and insert the plant. If you're planting seeds, you'll probably want to remove the plastic altogether.

22 **Use raised beds and floating row covers.** Among other advantages, raised beds catch the sunlight more intensely, and are always 5 to 6 degrees warmer than the surrounding ground. Floating row covers (see tip 162) provide extra warmth too. Although primarily intended as insect protection, they also warm the area underneath, and offer protection against unexpected frosts.

23 **Set out plants in bottomless black pots.** It's a certainty that you've accumulated a stack of one-gallon nursery pots made of black plastic. Here's a good use for them. With a sharp knife, cut away the bottom. In the garden, prepare for transplanting as usual, digging the hole a bit wider than the pot. Put your plant in the ground, as usual.

Now fit the black pot over the plant, pushing the edges down into the soil but leaving about half the height exposed. The black material will absorb heat, the plastic will act as a barrier to some pests, and the well you have created around the plant is a good way to irrigate deeply.

24 **Save your big coffee cans and plastic milk jugs.** Strip off the paper label from the cans, remove the bottom, and push the can down into the soil around baby plants. This helps protect seedlings from the cold and reflects light onto the plants. And if the weather forecast calls for very cold temperatures overnight, it's easy to add a plastic bag over the can and anchor it with a rubber band.

Also save your plastic milk jugs and make removable plant covers to protect against cold nights. Slice off the bottom completely (a sharp knife cuts easily through the plastic) but leave the top and the handle; the handle makes it easy to pick up and move the jug.

Cover the plant in the evening, pushing the edges of the jug down into the soil; remove when the temperature warms up. Unless it's really cold, unscrew the cap to allow for air circulation. When the need for them has passed, make a stack of jugs by slipping one inside another, and store them for next year.

25 **Use solar-heated water.** Set out buckets of water to catch the sun's rays. Use this warmed water directly around the roots of young plants, to warm the soil. Or stretch out the hose in a sunny spot; the water that first comes out will be quite warm. Careful: it can get scorching hot.

26 **Wood pallets make effective windbreaks.** Lean two together to make an A-frame over plants that need protection from wind. Because they are not solid, wind doesn't blow the pallets over, but they do a very effective job of dissipating the force of strong winds. Often warehouses and businesses in industrial parks give away slightly damaged pallets.

Another simple and movable windbreak can be made from burlap stretched over a frame. Old windows with the glass removed work well here; keep an eye out at yard sales. Both the pallets and the burlap "windows" also make nice sunscreens in the hot summer months.

27 **Build a permanent lean-to at the front of the garden.** Using poles or very long sturdy stakes, build an open structure (skeleton only, no walls) facing the garden. The poles at the front edge of the garden are set at a 45-degree angle, the tops lashed or nailed to vertical poles farther back. In the spring (and also fall), wrap the entire structure in clear plastic, stapling it to the poles, to create a sort-of greenhouse. When the weather warms up, roll the plastic aside. You can grow pole beans up the poles in summer.

If your garden is close to a building, you can accomplish the same thing even more easily by leaning poles against a wall that borders the garden. Wrap the area in spring, unwrap in summer.

◆28◆ Wrap the whole garden in plastic. You can get a serious jump on summer with this technique. Set aside one area, surround it with tall stakes, and encircle that entire area with plastic. Leave the top open for air circulation; cover it loosely if the temperature drops really low. Inside this temporary greenhouse, plant heat lovers like tomatoes, peppers, eggplant. This also is a good solution for those who live in an area where it never gets really hot (the coast, or high-elevation areas) but still want to grow warm-weather vegetables.

◆29◆ Gear up for working in the rain. Working in your garden when it's drizzling is a lot more bearable if you have the right personal gear. Designate a light rain jacket for garden work; it doesn't have to be pretty, so a good bargain from the thrift store is perfectly fine. Buy one of those rubber kneeling pads from the garden store to keep your jeans dry when you're down on your knees pulling weeds. Rubber boots for your feet; some people swear by garden clogs. And get some surgical gloves from the pharmacy; they'll keep your hands from getting muddy but fit tightly enough to allow you to work. And gear up your mindset too: we're *glad* for the rain, really we are.

Beating the Odds: Summer

30 **Install roll-up blinds along the garden fence.** Inexpensive bamboo or plastic blinds attach easily to the top crossbar of your fence and serve as good climate control all year long. You can lower them in summer to provide shade for heat-sensitive plants and prevent sunscald on really hot days, raise them to let sun through other times. Lower them on cold spring and fall days and nights to help create a protected environment, raise when the sun shines.

31 **In sunny country, summer gardens need mulch.** In northern California and east of the mountains throughout the Northwest, summertime weather can be very hot and dry. Add a bit of wind, and your soil will dry out and become crusted over in no time. Protect your plants with a thick layer of mulch to keep the soil cool and hold in moisture: straw, pine needles, oak leaves, or any kind of chopped-up vegetation.

32 **Prepare some kind of shade protection and have it at the ready.** Wherever you live in the Northwest, there comes a time when you have to think about protecting your plants from hot sun. On the dry eastern side, it's all summer long, and you may want something semipermanent, like posts supporting shade cloth stretched over the garden plot. West of the mountains, the best approach is something light and portable that you can move in and out as need be.

Here are several possibilities: Put several waist-high stakes around the perimeter of the garden and stretch an old sheet over them, fastening with strong rubber bands. Buy nursery shade cloth (available at large garden centers and nursery supply houses) and stretch it over wooden frames, like stretching canvas for a painting. Set the frames over the plants, supported on sawhorses or old tomato cages.

Old aluminum window screens (pick them up whenever you see them at garage sales) are lightweight and easily moved; prop them against stakes set at an angle. Other shade tricks: the burlap screens and pallets described in tip 26 and the roll-up blinds from tip 30.

33 **In warmer areas, rely on trench planting.** In northern California and Banana Belt areas of Oregon and Washington (if you live in one, you know who you are), where summer temperatures can get scorching hot, use trench planting (see tip 20). Because hot air rises, the bottoms of the trenches are a few degrees cooler.

34 **If you're planting seeds for the fall garden, keep the area moist.** You need to put your seeds into the ground in plenty of time for them to be up and ready for October and November, which could mean you're planting in August, when the ground is hot and dry– good for the beans and squash that are already producing, not good for germinating. So keep the seed-bed constantly damp. This may mean watering it every day.

Another way, which also helps the soil from crusting over, is to cover the seeded area with peat moss, straw, even a wet burlap bag; keep it damp with a light spray.

35 **Protect tall summer crops from wind.** Wind can be particularly distressing in late summer when tall vulnerable plants like corn and indeterminate tomatoes are at their peak. One good way to battle wind is to build a "fence" horizontally over these crops. While the plants are still young, put stakes about 4 feet high around the area and attach wide-mesh wire fencing to the tops of the stakes, parallel to the ground. The plants will grow up through it, and the fencing will hold them upright. Just be sure to select something with a grid wide enough for a cornstalk.

Beating the Odds: Fall

36 **Reinstate your portable frost protection devices from springtime.** The maritime areas are blessed with basically mild weather up till early December, but days get shorter and night temperatures drop. You want to let in all the sun that's available during the day and protect against coolness at night. So bring out the plastic and the floating row covers; cover up, let the shades down, mulch up, and heed the weather forecast for frost.

In the valley areas, the most common weather pattern is an early burst of cool weather, followed by another period of Indian summer. Be ready to cover the frost-sensitive plants with plastic or even an old sheet until the warm weather returns.

37 **Use reflective panels to balance light.** As the sun gets lower in the sky, any shady areas of your garden get even shadier and plants lean toward the sun. Make portable panels out of heavy cardboard, hardboard, or thin plywood. Paint them white or cover with aluminum foil, and stand them up at strategic points to reflect light back toward plants.

38 **Cover raised beds with plastic stretched over hoops.** Raised beds are always a bit warmer than the surrounding areas, and if you provide some overhead protection against cool weather, you can continue to grow summer crops into the fall. Bend narrow PVC pipe into hoops a bit taller than your tallest plants, then cover the entire bed with plastic or floating row cover. (Works in spring too, of course.)

Beating the Odds: Winter

39 **Cover empty vegetable beds with a heavy blanket of yard debris.** Rake up all the leaves, spread them out in a thin pile to dry, and run the lawn mower over to chop them up. Do the same with vegetable plants that have finished producing, or annual flowers past their season. Save grass clippings. Collect pine needles. Whatever vegetative material you can get your hands on, spread it out on garden plots that are going to be empty till spring. All this stuff will gradually break down during the winter, doing terrific things for your soil.

40 **Protect large winter vegetable plants with leaf pillows.** Fill black plastic bags loosely with dry leaves or pine needles. Squeeze out the extra air and tie tightly at the top. The bag can now be molded around the base of plants, providing a form of insulation against periods of heavy cold. The black plastic keeps the leaves from deteriorating in the rain, and will absorb whatever heat is available. You can save the bags from year to year, or start new ones each fall.

41 **Many root crops can stay right in the garden.** If you cover them with a thick mulch, beets, carrots, and turnips can stay right where they are through the winter. The tops may die down, so you might need a marker to help you remember where they are. And some of the leafy vegetables can keep through the winter as well; Swiss chard is just about foolproof.

42 **Use empty tomato cages as compost bins.** When the tomato plants have been taken up, move the empty cages to various spots in the garden area. During the winter months, fill them with compost materials. Come spring, just lift off the cage and spread the compost around.

43 **In northern California, take advantage of your weather.** In winter, your days are longer and usually warmer. Most years, you can grow many things right through the winter: lettuce, spinach, chard, all the brassicas, scallions, radishes, turnips, snow peas.

FROM THE GROUND UP

❧ ❧ ❧

Compost and Other Soil Amendments

44 **Compost is a miracle worker for all kinds of Northwest soils.** Compost not only provides nutrients to the soil, it significantly improves its texture. If you live in the western regions of the Northwest, you probably have heavy clay soil that water doesn't drain through; compost will lighten it up. If you live on the east side of the mountains, your soil probably is sandy and alkaline; compost will add body, so soil holds water better.

45 **You don't really need a formal compost bin.** An actual compost bin, where you layer soil and organic debris and sprinkle with water, is the way to go if you want to produce large quantities of compost. But there are easier ways, and they are almost as effective.

Lazy compost: save your kitchen scraps (no meat) in a small bucket, when it's full take it out to the garden, dig a hole, dump it in, cover up the hole. Done.

You can continue this right through the winter, even in areas where the ground freezes, with this trick: In autumn, after the leaves have fallen but before the first hard freeze, dig a series of holes in your vegetable garden and fill them with leaves or pine needles. During the winter, pull up the leaves, dump in the contents of your bucket, cover with the leaves.

You will get faster results (material breaks down more quickly) if you make "compost soup": Put vegetable peelings, coffee grounds, eggshells, but not meat products, in a blender. Add enough water to make a liquid. Pour the slush into small holes in the vegetable beds. Search yard sales or thrift stores for a good used blender and set it aside just for this purpose.

46 **Ashes from the fireplace provide potash (potassium).** They also contain calcium, magnesium, and a trace amount of phosphorus; all in all, a free source of important nutrients. When you clean out your fireplace or woodstove, save the ashes. Spread them over the garden an inch or so thick, till into the soil in the early spring.

47 **Eggshells and shellfish shells are a good source of calcium.** And calcium is good for all growing plants (forms strong cells). Save eggshells and let them dry thoroughly, then crush them thoroughly. A small handful in the bottom of the planting hole provides calcium to tomato plants and helps prevent blossom end rot later on.

Shells from shrimp and crabs are another good source of calcium, although a bit harder to crush up. Feed stores sell large bags of crushed oyster shells; they're intended for chickens, but work just as well tilled into the garden as a calcium supplement. One application will last for years.

48 **Blended citrus peels will acidify alkaline soil.** In the eastern regions of the Northwest states, where annual rainfall is low, soils tend to be dry and excessively alkaline. Soil for vegetables should have a balanced pH level, midway between acidic and alkaline, so eastern gardeners need to add acid. A free source is the peels of oranges, lemons, and limes. Chop them in the garden blender (see tip 45), add water to make slush, and pour it around the garden.

Starting from Seed

49 **Starting your own seed gives you more control.** Whether to start from seed or from purchased transplants is one of those maddening questions that has no one right answer. Arguments for seed: (1) You know what you're getting. (2) Considering all the delicious things offered in catalogs, you have a much wider range of options, including exotic varieties you'll never find in the typical garden center. (3) In some cases you have no choice. Some things just don't transplant well, like peas and beans (except see tip 112); some things you won't find for sale as transplants, like carrots and beets. Arguments against: (1) It's less convenient. (2) It takes space and attention. (3) If you do it right, you end up with a *lot* of seedlings.

50 **Consolidate your seed orders with a friend.** One way to get around the problem of having too many seeds is to double up with a buddy, each of you taking half a packet. Or use just what you want from your packets and donate the rest to the garden coordinator at your local community garden. Or offer them to a daycare center as a kids' project; add some of those used 2-inch pots you've been saving and now have a million of.

51 Start seeds directly in peat pots to avoid transplant shock later.

For things you want to start indoors early, put one seed into a 2-inch peat pot full of seedling mix. Use commercial seed-starting mix, which is very porous and completely sterile. You may need a tweezer to make sure you get just one seed. When it's ready to go outside, you put the whole thing in the ground, pot and all.

An alternative is a peat pellet, which starts out flat like a half-dollar and expands in water; use the new type that doesn't have a string shell, and you won't have to worry about digging the string out of your soil someday.

If your baby plant outgrows the peat pot before the weather is ready for outdoor planting, pot it up into something larger for the holding period; again, just put the entire peat pot into, say, a 4-inch pot and fill in with potting mix.

52 **Don't be in a rush.** The seed catalogs arrive in January, and you send in your order in February, and the seeds arrive soon after. The pictures make your mouth water, and you can't wait to get started. Wait anyway. If you start the seeds too early, you'll get leggy plants that just keep on getting taller and spindlier, and by the time the weather is right for putting them out, they've lost all vigor.

Some seeds are ready to go outside in two weeks, many others take just three to four weeks, and only tomatoes and peppers take six weeks. Pay attention to germination times (listed on the seed packet) and to frost dates (see tip 18), especially for hot-weather vegetables, and backtime accordingly.

These are the easiest seeds to start indoors: cucumbers, squash, melons, lettuce, chives, broccoli, cauliflower, cabbage.

53 **Use your ingenuity to create seedling containers.** You can buy fancy modular systems for seed-starting, but they're designed for commercial nurseries and others who do large-volume plantings. For a back-yard garden, you'll save money, and feel virtuous, if you recycle things that pass through your life anyway. In the environmentally righteous Northwest, inspiration is everywhere.

For instance: My favorite Vietnamese restaurant uses two-part takeout containers that have a black plastic bottom and a clear plastic top. They make perfect little greenhouses; the black collects heat, the clear top lets light through. I punch holes in the bottom for drainage, and set the whole thing on one of those foam trays that supermarkets use to package fresh meat.

◆54◆ When seeding directly in the garden, follow directions and keep seeds damp. The seed packet will tell you how far apart to put the seeds and how deeply; pay attention.

Cover newly planted seeds with damp peat moss. It will keep the surface damp until seeds germinate, and is much safer than continual watering, which has a distressing tendency to wash the seeds away. It also provides a weed-free environment. If the seeds take a long time to germinate, cover the peat moss with damp newspaper or burlap to prevent its drying out and blowing away.

Starting with Baby Plants

◆55◆ Buying potted seedlings from a garden center gives you a good head start. Starting with "starts" is convenient and saves you being over-run with more seedlings that you can use. But the main reason for starting with baby plants is, it's a good way to get a jump on the short growing season that most Northwesterners have to deal with. Someone else—a commercial grower who's better equipped than you are—has already pampered the plant through the first few difficult weeks of growth, has already fought the fungus, has already lost half the seedlings to slugs.

56 **If you start your own seedlings indoors, give them a good transition.** Don't go straight from your warm kitchen window to cool outdoors; make the move in gradual steps, with an interim period on the back porch or a protected outside area. This is known as hardening off, and it's especially important in the Northwest, where the weather at planting time can change so suddenly.

57 **Give young transplants a boost with a mild fertilizer.** A good technique is to fill a bucket with a weak solution of fish emulsion or some other organic fertilizer. Take the young plant from its container and put the whole thing, soil and all, into the liquid. Let it soak there and loosen up while you dig the hole it's going into. After all the transplants are in the ground, pour the contents of the bucket around them.

Smart Watering

58 **Face it—you need to water your garden in the summer.** Those who live in the western parts of the Northwest tend to get lulled into thinking they don't need to irrigate the garden because it rains so much. In summer, skies may be overcast and it *looks* like rain but the soil is becoming very dried out. Once the plants lose internal moisture, they are permanently set back. Don't be stubborn about this.

59 **Water the soil, not the air.** Most of the water from oscillating sprinklers is lost to evaporation. Of the rest, some falls on the leaves of the plants and creates conditions that promote mildew and fungal diseases, especially when the weather is cool, which it often is as late in June in the Northwest. A much better approach is to water the soil directly.

Moving the hose from one spot to another is one way, and it's not too inconvenient if you're already in the garden for a work session. Another way is to dig shallow trenches near the plants (this is easier if you have planted things in rows) and fill the trenches with water.

60 **Soaker hoses plus a mulch make the most efficient watering system of all.** Soaker hoses release water all along their length; they come in two general styles. One is a flattened plastic hose with tiny holes all along the sides; you place it around the garden close to plants. The other type is made from recycled tires; the surface is porous, so that water continuously seeps out in beads of moisture like dew. Snake it through the garden in an S pattern, burying it underground a little.

Best of all, place soaker hoses around the garden bed, cover the entire bed with a mulch, and leave everything in place. You can combine as many lengths as you need. The end of the last soaker hose attaches to your regular garden hose, so you can unscrew it as needed. This kind of system is especially effective in dry regions east of the mountains.

61 **Water only when necessary, and do it thoroughly.** It's the roots of the plants that need the water, not the surface of the soil. A good solid soak once a week is much, much better than a puny dribble once a day.

Rule of thumb: you want to get the soil wet 6 inches down. That will take a solid inch of water, and that takes about 3 hours with a sprinkler, depending on your water pressure. To be sure how much your sprinkler puts out, set out an empty shallow pan or tuna can and measure the water as it fills.

Even that may not tell you everything. Some plants with large leaves (squash, for instance) actually block water from the ground right around the roots (another argument for a soaker system). Dig down 6 inches or so at several different spots in the garden to see if things are really wet.

62 **Plant new seedlings inside a moat.** Whenever you put new transplants into the ground, take some of the dirt you dug out and form a walled moat in a circle around the plant. With your hose, fill up the moat and water will go straight to the plant's roots, rather than all over the place. This is especially helpful with heavy clay soil.

63 **Perforated cans or milk jugs deliver water deeply to one specific spot.** A large juice can or 3-pound coffee can with several holes in the sides and bottom makes a very efficient way to get water down to the roots. This is especially valuable with very heavy clay soil, which might otherwise be hard for water to penetrate.

Push the can down into the soil close to plants, leaving an inch or so exposed at the top. Fill the can with water, and it will gradually escape through the holes. You can also add liquid fertilizer this way. Or fill the bottom with a few inches of manure and top off the can with water, for a slow release of manure tea. It's best to sink these cans while the plants are very young, so you don't run the risk of breaking roots.

A similar idea uses gallon plastic milk jugs. Punch several holes all around the sides and bottom. Bury the jug, leaving just the top above the surface. Plant several smallish plants in a circle around the jug, like lettuce, spinach, or bush beans. All through the growing period, you'll be able to get plenty of water right where it's needed, and fertilizer too, by filling the jug. The advantage of the milk jug over the tin can is that its narrow top minimizes evaporation.

A BOUNTY OF VEGETABLES

❦ ❦ ❦

Beans

64 **Bean basics, varieties.** Pole beans grow like a vine and need some sort of support. Bush beans are short bushy plants, one to two feet high, that don't need extra support. Pole beans take longer to develop the first beans, but then produce over a long period of time. Bush beans reach maturity faster but have a smaller crop, and pretty much all at once. That's one of life's trade-offs.

Beans are a summertime crop; they grow well only when both daytime and nighttime temperatures are warm. In the fickle Northwest weather, some years you may have to hold off first planting till June.

Popular varieties of bush beans include Tendercrop, wonderful fresh but doesn't can well; Yellow Wax, a nice yellow bean that is very prolific; and the classic Blue Lake, good fresh and canned. All take approximately 55 days. Good varieties of pole beans are Kentucky Wonder (60 to 70 days) and Cascade Giant (65 to 70 days), developed at Oregon State University by Dr. James Baggett. The truth is, almost all beans do well in western Oregon and Washington; many of the canned beans found on grocery shelves nationwide were grown and harvested in the Willamette Valley.

◆65◆ Stagger plantings for extended season. Start with a fast-maturing bush bean as soon as the ground is truly warm (mid-May, if you're lucky). About two weeks later, plant pole beans. A few weeks after that, sow another crop of bush beans. That should give you a continuous supply of fresh beans from the end of June through October. If you don't have a way to grow pole beans, you can accomplish much the same effect with just bush beans by staggering the planting. Every ten days or so, put in a few seeds; that way, you won't have to deal with a full crop all coming ready at the same time.

66 **Don't soak seeds before plant-ing.** The seed seems rock-hard but readily absorbs ground moisture. If you soak the seed first, it may expand too fast and blast open, destroying the embryo in the process. Best technique: thoroughly water the ground one day, plant seeds the next day without additional watering. Also applies to peas.

Beets

67 **Beet basics, varieties.** Beets produce two crops: the underground round red root, which is what most people mean when they think of a beet, and the aboveground leaves, which only home gardeners get to enjoy. Beet greens are extremely nutritious and have a softer, mellower flavor than many other table greens. And not all beets are red; you can grow yellow and orange varieties—something else only home gardeners can do.

Beets grow best when the weather is coolish, and do poorly in hot summer. For a long harvest, plant early for a spring crop and then again in late summer for a fall crop.

The rough, irregular beet seed is actually a hardened cluster of seeds, so when it germinates, several tiny seedlings come up very close together. As soon as they are established (with two true leaves), thin these seedlings.

The classic beet is Detroit Dark Red (60 days), which does well virtually anywhere; the greens are tender and delicious. Cylindra (60 days) is shaped like a short, fat carrot; this cylindrical shape permits nice even slices, and so it is a good choice for pickled beets. Kids (and beet-reluctant adults) will enjoy Chioggias, with their colorful red and white circles on the inside.

68 **Pay attention to water, especially in summer.** The trick to developing sweet, tender beets (the red part) is to make sure the roots are consistently getting plenty of water while they are actively growing. Dry soil, or alternating periods of wet and dry, will produce hard, woody roots. Your spring crop could be maturing during hot days of summer, so be sure to water deeply and often.

Broccoli

69 **Broccoli basics, varieties.** Broccoli is a cool-weather plant that tends to bolt in hot summer but does quite well in spring and fall—which makes it practically perfect for the Northwest, where spring seems interminable and fall often lasts until past Thanksgiving. The part we eat, called the curd, is actually a fat cluster of immature flower buds. Harvest when the heads are still tight; once they begin to fatten up, they're almost ready to flower, and the first hot day they'll open up so fast you won't believe it.

Green Comet (55 days from transplants) is a reliable producer of medium-size heads. Emperor Hybrid (65 days) takes a little longer but makes larger heads. Packman (55 days) is a good "branching" type. Another, called Purple Sprouting, is hardy, usually winters over.

70 **To make good heads, broccoli needs to grow fast.** To do that, it needs consistent watering, rich soil, good drainage, and a boost of nitrogen. Be careful, though; too much nitrogen will produce hollow stems. In western Oregon and Washington, you'll probably need to add lime to the soil. Also, be vigilant about aphids and caterpillars; any plant with so much succulent new growth is very attractive to aphids.

71 **Sprouting broccoli lasts all season.** Most years, you can get two full crops—one in spring, one in fall—if you time your planting carefully. But a simpler way to have a continuous supply of broccoli is to plant a branching, or sprouting, variety. These produce a central head, like the others, but after it is cut off, they grow smaller heads sideways from the stem, at the leaf axils. If you keep harvesting them, more will form, and you can get a whole year's harvest from one planting. That is, if you can keep it from bolting; most of the branching varieties are also bolt-resistant, but not foolproof.

Brussels Sprouts

72 **Brussels sprouts basics, varieties.** Like its brassica cousins, this plant requires rich soil, consistent watering, and regular feedings of fertilizer that is high in nitrogen. The part we eat, which looks like cabbages in miniature, forms in the angle between leaf and stem, tight up against the stem. For best flavor, pick them when they're small. For fresh eating, harvest a few at a time, starting from the bottom.

The two standard varieties are Jade Cross (85 days from transplants) and Prince Marvel (95 days). Except for the growing time, they're pretty much the same.

73 **Brussels sprouts like cold weather.** This vegetable is prized by many northwesterners because it is not bothered by very cold weather. In fact, a light frost improves the flavor, makes the sprouts sweeter.

That means that when most everything else has been done in by winter weather, you can still get a nice dish of Brussels sprouts.

The flip side is that hot weather, even the lush days of Indian summer, encourage aphids, which already consider Brussels sprouts nirvana because of all the new growth. Check carefully for early signs of aphids; hose them off whenever you can and, when that doesn't work, use an insecticidal soap every two weeks or so. There's nothing worse than cutting into a beautiful butter-steamed sprout and finding it full of yucky dead black things.

Cabbage

74 **Cabbage basics, varieties.** Cabbage is often considered the queen of the cole crops, and shares the family traits: it's a fairly heavy feeder, likes consistent watering and limey soil, and does best in cooler weather. Stonehead (50 days from transplants) makes a small head that's a good size for a small family. Ruby Ball (65 days) is a red cabbage that produces a firm, medium head. Dutch Flat is an old favorite for late-season crops.

75 **Expand your cabbage horizons.** The familiar green garden cabbage we all know and love is full of vitamin C, is easy to grow, and makes great coleslaw. But there's more to the cabbage world. You probably already know red cabbage (it's no more difficult to grow) but you may not be acquainted with some other options. Oriental varieties like Chinese cabbage, bok choy, and mizuna are fast-growing spring plants; you can harvest just a few outside leaves without taking up the whole plant. Savoy cabbage, with its pretty ruffled leaves, is less bothered by hot weather than regular cabbage.

76 Leave the stalk in the ground to make babies. Instead of yanking the whole plant from the ground, cut off the main head but leave the stalk in place. Trim away any very large outside leaves, continue to water the plant, and eventually several small heads will form along the stalk. They'll never become grown-ups, but will reach a tidy one-serving size.

77 Leave cabbage in the ground to prolong the harvest. One mature head produces a *lot* of cabbage; ten plants all coming ready at the same time can be completely overwhelming. Let Mother Nature store them for you, with this technique. Grab the head with both hands and twist the whole plant a quarter turn. Don't lift upward, just turn. This will rupture some of the side roots so the plant stops growing, but the taproot is not affected, so the plant remains alive and crisp for several more weeks.

Carrots

78 **Carrot basics, varieties.** Carrots can be slow to germinate, and they're difficult to grow in heavy clay soil—both solvable. Otherwise, there's no mystery to this garden favorite. Pioneer produces a reliable winter crop; Danvers Half-Long and Chantenay are shorter, work well in heavy soils.

79 **Choose midget varieties.** The long, skinny tapers we are accustomed to seeing in the grocery store are very hard to grow in the heavy clay soil that most northwesterners have to contend with; they get twisted and contorted trying to grow through the soil—that is, if the root maggots don't get them first or if they don't rot during the long growing period.

The smaller thumb-size or radish-shaped varieties are sweeter, reach eating size faster, and need only a few inches of good growing soil. And you'll have a delicious treat you could never find at the supermarket.

80 **Sow carrot seeds mixed with sand.** Carrot seeds are very small. This makes it difficult to sow them evenly, which means you'll have a tedious thinning job later. One way to spread the seeds more thinly is to first mix them with a handful of sand, which has the effect of physically separating the seeds. An extra benefit: the sand will help improve drainage in the soil, which is important for carrots.

81 **Sow twice.** Plant seeds in early spring for a summer crop; in early summer for a fall or winter crop. The second crop can stay in the ground through the winter; mulch well with straw or leaves to protect against freezing, and pull a few as needed. If you mulch several areas, leave yourself some kind of marker to distinguish where the carrots are.

82 **Germination tricks, indoors and out.** Speed up germination by covering the sown ground with damp burlap. Or soak seeds indoors and roll them up in a damp paper towel until they break open, then plant.

You can also get a head start on the spring crop by starting seeds indoors. In whatever seed-starting medium you prefer, poke about ten small holes and put one seed in each. After they germinate, put the whole clump in the ground. As they grow, they'll bump into each other, forcing the outermost carrots outward. Pull out a few at a young eating stage, and the ones that remain will fill in the now-empty spaces.

Cauliflower

83 **Cauliflower basics, varieties.** Another member of the charming and nourishing brassica family, cauliflower needs what all its cousins need: coolish weather, abundant moisture, limey soil, good drainage, and nitrogen-rich fertilizer. In the Pacific Northwest, the first two come free; you'll probably have to make an effort to provide the remaining three. The part we eat is rather unappetizingly called the curd; it's white if you take specific measures to keep it so.

Early Snowball is the standard; several related varieties have more specific names. All take about 55 days from transplants, and all have extra-large leaves to provide the cover-up that keeps the curds white. Purple varieties (Sicilian Purple, Violet Queen) don't have to be covered up, for the colored curd (which turns green when cooked) is part of the charm.

84 **Use the leaves to blanch the heads.** White cauliflower is white because it never sees the sun. If left exposed, the curds turn a muddy and decidedly unappetizing yellow. To keep them white, pull the large outer leaves up and over the developing head, and tie them or pin them together with clothespins. All-natural option: take a short, straight, stiff twig and use it like a straight pin.

85 **Don't dally getting plants in.** As soon as the first set of true leaves forms, put the transplants into the ground. If left in your windowsill or greenhouse pots too long, they will start to form a head. It's what the plant genetically wants to do, but it's too soon. This tiny head is called a button, and it effectively freezes the plant's growth at that point.

86 **Stagger your plantings.** You don't want all your cauliflower to be ready in the same week (unless you're feeding the whole neighborhood). So put in two or three transplants at weekly intervals, backtiming from the last killing frost. If you start seeds yourself, you'll have to stagger that process too, to avoid buttoning (see tip 85). Or buy baby plants on two separate trips to the garden center.

Corn

87 **Corn basics, varieties.** In home gardens corn takes a lot of space and a lot of water, but if you love the taste of real corn you'll happily make the sacrifice. Northwesterners take on even greater liability: the really hot weather that corn needs may peter out before harvest is ready; nonetheless, we persist, for the rewards are sweet indeed.

Corn is a hot-weather vegetable and germinates only when the soil has warmed up. It's also a heavy feeder; before planting, work in a goodly measure of compost or well-rotted manure and continue to fertilize regularly during early growth period. Birds love the young sprouts; floating row covers help.

"Sweet corn" is the generic name for what most of us mean when we say corn, to distinguish from varieties that make popcorn or brightly colored decorative ears. Sweet corn is available in three general types: "regular" hybrids, with kernels that are yellow, white, or a mix of both; supersweet hybrids, genetically engineered for double sweetness that turns to starch more slowly; and sugar-enhanced hybrids, which fall somewhere between those two extremes, a compromise between extra sweetness and old-fashioned flavor. All three kinds come in a range of maturities; altogether, enough choices to make you dizzy. Comparative catalog study is important here.

Early Sunglow (62 days, regular hybrid) is a wonderful choice for the Northwest; it matures early and, given sufficient water and warmth, is very reliable. Keeps well on the stalk or in the refrigerator. Golden Jubilee (85 days) is the classic variety; this is what you will find in markets and roadside stands; there is a supersweet version of Jubilee, too.

88 **Soak the seeds first.** Before you plant corn seeds, soak them first in warm water, for a few hours or overnight. This helps them germinate faster. In our climate, where true summertime can be very short, anything you do to jump-start those vegetables that need a long summer season is worth doing.

89 **Plant a rectangular plot of short rows.** Corn is pollinated by wind, and full pollination is what makes full, plump ears with no bare spots. The wind blowing crosswise across a long straight row blows pollen out into nothingness; across multiple short rows, wind from any direction will blow pollen onto other corn plants.

90 **Be aggressive to control corn earworm.** Those curly little devils will ruin the top part of any ear they get into. The trick is to keep out the moth that lays the eggs that turn into the larvae that eat your corn before you do. One technique is to tie small paper bags loosely over the tops of the developing ears.

Another is to dab a few drops of oil on the tip just where the silk comes out; you can use vegetable oil, mineral oil, even baby oil. Or plant varieties that mature early; in most parts of the Northwest, the moths don't come calling until late summer, so if you've already had your harvest, they have no reason to stick around.

Cucumbers

91 **Cucumber basics, varieties.** Cucumbers need only two things to flourish: hot weather, and lots of water. Once those are provided, the plants grow so vigorously that any pests (principally, the cucumber beetle) do little damage. You can start with either seeds or transplants; there is some evidence that transplants do slightly better. Most people who seed directly into the ground plant several seeds together in a cluster (called a hill) and thin the seedlings down to the two or three strongest ones.

Most catalogs distinguish between slicing (that is, "eating") and pickling varieties; the difference is the mature size of the cucumbers. All kinds of cukes do well in the Northwest, as long as you give them ample water; here are some longtime favorites. Liberty, a pickling cucumber, is very prolific, and makes fruits of consistent size (important for attractive jars). Marketmore and Straight 8 are very reliable slicing cucumbers. Lemon cucumbers are round and yellow, instead of long and green, and quite delicious.

Most cucumber plants have separate male and female flowers and require some pollination assistance from your friends the honeybees. Some newer varieties are self-pollinating but otherwise basically the same.

◇92◇ Provide some kind of trellis support. There are bush-type cucumbers available, but most of what you will find for sale is the vine type. They can either sprawl on the ground, which seems easier on the gardener but in the long run is not, or climb up some kind of supporting structure, which is actually much better for the cukes.

If you let the vines grow along the ground, the plants are more susceptible to disease and mold and the cucumbers themselves often rot on the bottom. If you grow them on some kind of vertical support, you provide much better air circulation, which helps prevent disease. Growing cucumbers vertically has three other advantages: you get more use out of your space, you get nice straight cucumbers, and you're much less likely to step on them.

93 **Help the soil warm up.** Cucumbers simply won't grow until both air and soil temperatures are really warm—which can be a problem in the Northwest, where cool June nights are not at all uncommon. You can help things along by warming up the soil. Cover a section of the garden bed with plastic; cut a slit or X for the baby plants.

Another way to raise the temperature of the soil is to make a small mound and put your seed or transplant on top; soil that is raised up even a few inches is warmer than the adjacent ground. Best of all: do both.

94 **Keep the area well watered.** Cucumbers need a *lot* of water. Their root system is shallow; there is no taproot to pull moisture from deep in the soil, so you need to water them well and consistently. If you used plastic around the plants, leave it in place and run your hose underneath; the plastic helps keep the soil from drying out so fast. This is the whole secret for mild-tasting, unbitter cukes: keep them growing fast with lots of water and occasional fertilizer. And of course pick them before they get big and tough.

Garlic

95 **Garlic basics, varieties.** The whole garlic bulb, the one we find in the supermarket next to the onions, is a cluster of 20 or so cloves. Each clove, planted into the ground in the fall, will grow an entire new bulb by the following spring. And in the meantime your home will be safe from vampires.

All garlics do equally well in the Northwest. For fun, try Top Set, which makes small bulbs on the top of each plant; and Elephant garlic, with humongous bulbs that can weigh more than a pound but have a surprisingly mild taste.

96 **Growing and harvesting garlic.** Plant garlic in the fall, before the ground freezes. Holes should be 5 inches deep; plant the clove vertically, with the more pointed end up. In cold climates, mulch the spot well. That's all there is to it. When the green tops show in summer, start watching. Don't let the plants flower and go to seed. Cut off any seed heads that form. This will help the plant form a cluster of cloves instead of one big bulb.

About July, the green tops will have turned to brown. That's your signal that the bulbs are ready to harvest. Use a spading fork rather than a shovel; you're less likely to cut a bulb in half. Spread bulbs somewhere dry and warm for a few days; right in the garden is fine. For longest storage, set them in the shade for several days for a final curing.

If you want to make a garlic braid, do so while the brown tops are still pliable, or soak in water the day before. Hang the finished braid outdoors for two months, to dry thoroughly. Inside, store at about 60°F; if the temperature drops below 50, they start to sprout.

Greens

97 **Greens basics, varieties.** In this category are grouped together a wide range of greens that are less well known than lettuce and spinach (which have their own listings)—things like kale, Swiss chard, collards, mustard greens, and the many wonderful oriental leafy vegetables. They have many things in common: they are easy to grow, exceptionally nutritious, and not particularly attractive to pests. They grow blissfully in cool weather and so make excellent spring and fall crops; in fact, many live right through the winter in low-elevation parts of the Northwest, and frost improves their taste. As a group they are also very attractive; this, together with a compact growing habit, makes them good candidates for container gardening.

Virtually all varieties do acceptably well in the Northwest. Rather than recommending a specific variety, instead I recommend you have fun studying the catalogs and try something that is brand-new to you. Almost every garden has room for a few of these vitamin factories.

Lettuce

98 **Lettuce basics, varieties.** Lettuce is a cool-season plant, which makes it ideal for most Northwest climates. It grows best in spring and fall, which we have lots of, and horribly in summertime heat, which we have little of. In fact, once the temperature gets above 80°F, lettuce seed will not germinate. You'll have more consistent success if you start seeds indoors, starting in very early spring.

Once in the garden, lettuce doesn't need a lot of pampering—although you will have to be watchful of slugs in the spring—except for one thing: watering. Dry soil is what makes lettuce taste bitter; water often to keep the plants growing fast, for sweet, tender lettuce. If you still have plants in the garden in July and August, give them as much shade as you can.

There are hundreds of types of lettuce, which can be loosely grouped into two overall categories: heading and looseleaf. Some catalogs further subdivide the "heading" category into butterheads, crispheads, romaines, bibbs, etc. Looseleaf lettuces do not form a head per se, but grow in a loose cluster of individual leaves; you can harvest just a few leaves as you need them, and the plant keeps growing. Almost all looseleaf types do well in the Northwest; Oak Leaf (50 days) comes in both red and green varieties, and tolerates hot weather better than most. Among the crispheads, Summertime (70 days) is a smashing success. A romaine type developed by Dr. Baggett at OSU, it is slow to bolt, keeps well in the garden over a long time, and never seems to taste bitter.

99 **Lettuce will bolt: accept it.** One day your lettuce plant looks nice and normal; the next day (or so it seems) it has suddenly shot up to three feet high, with the leaves widely stretched out along a fat stalk and a flower head forming on the top. That's bolting. And there's very little you can do about it. When the weather turns hot, lettuce will bolt, period. The romaine types handle hot weather best, and some varieties of the other types are specially bred to be heat-tolerant. If you hope to grow lettuce in the summer you should definitely search them out.

If some bolt on you anyway, let it happen. The flowers are attractive to bees, and then you can save your own seed for next year. If the scraggly look of bolted plants bothers you, yank the whole thing up and add it to your compost pile. Or use the elongated plants as mulch around other vegetables.

⟨100⟩ Lettuce is a good vegetable for fall gardens. After the hot summer weather ruins your spring lettuce crop, start some more seedlings for fall. They'll be ready to go into the ground in a few weeks. By then, the hot weather may have passed and you'll be heading toward fall, a time of year that makes lettuces very happy. Remember that seeds don't germinate when the weather is warm, so look for an area in your house that's somewhat cool. If you're doing all this when the air temperature is really hot, try this trick: put the packet of seeds in the freezer overnight. Next day, plant as usual.

Melons

101 **Melon basics, varieties.** In maritime climates (coastal California and western Oregon and Washington), growing melons is a definite challenge. They need hot weather and lots of it; and they take up huge amounts of space. If you live in one of those areas, don't even bother with the larger melons like the traditional watermelons—there won't be enough warm sunny days for fruit to mature. If you have the room, though, there's nothing like the sweet flavor of vine-ripened cantaloupe. East of the Cascades, almost all melons do well. Two cantaloupe for western regions are Harper Hybrid and Hale's Best.

102 **Keep the soil warm and wet.** Success with melons means two things: a warm and very rich soil and lots of water. Best technique: dig in lots of compost early in season; at planting time, cover melon bed with black plastic, cut slits in the plastic and put a seedling in that spot. Then once a week run your hose underneath to water thoroughly. Add fish emulsion or some other organic fertilizer regularly.

103 **Build a special box for grow-**
ing melons. If you want to get
really serious about melons, here's one
way to get a jump on our late-arriving
summer: build one of Peter Chan's
melon boxes.

Using 2 x 2 lumber, frame a box about
2 feet square and 6 feet high. Add cedar fence boards for the sides, up to
about 2 feet from the ground. Add hori-
zontal crosspieces of 2 x 2 at the top.
Now you have a solid but bottomless
box 2 feet high topped with a 4-foot trellis. Add two layers of chicken wire on
the bottom to keep out gophers, then
fill in with compost-enriched soil. Add
string from the top of the solid wall to
the top of the trellis crosspieces, so
melons have something to climb on.

When you first plant the seedlings,
cover the entire trellis frame with clear
plastic to create a warm environment.
As the weather begins to heat up, pull
some of the plastic aside to provide air
circulation and cover again for the
night. In the dead of summer, remove
the plastic completely but keep it handy
for a sudden cold night.

104 **When the melons develop,**
keep them up off the ground.
If the melons are sitting on the ground,
especially wet ground, they are susceptible to rot. Lift them up off the soil with
a small "pillow" of straw or dried leaves.

Or set them on top of an empty tuna can. (Same for large winter squash, too.) When the melon is softball-size, cut back on watering; the melon will have much richer flavor. Water only when the weather is so hot the vines start to wilt.

Onions

105 **Onion basics, varieties.** The big fat slicing onions are called "bulb" onions; the part we eat is either white, yellow, or red, and grows underground. The other kind, grown for the green tops as well as the very slender underground white onion, are called green onions, bunching onions, or scallions. You can, if you want, use the green tops of bulb onions or harvest the onions when they are very young as scallions, but that rather defeats the purpose.

Bulb onions need a long growing period to make a real bulb; most people buy seedlings to get a jump on things. Scallions grow fast and can be direct-seeded into the ground. Both need lots of water.

For bulb onions, if you live in the Northwest you *have* to grow Walla Walla sweets, or the onion police will come after you. You'll want to anyway: they're easy to grow here (80 days from transplants), and their sweet, mild taste is world-famous. Ebenezer (100 days) stores very well over the winter.

◆106◆ **Keep flower heads pinched out, and weed meticulously.** If the plant goes to flower, the underground bulb won't form well. Your main task when growing onions is to keep weeds away. More than most crops, onions cannot tolerate the competition for water. Onions also like a dose of high-nitrogen fertilizer.

Onions are ready to harvest when the tops start to fall over. Spread them on newspapers in the shade for several days until the neck is soft, the skins are papery, and the root hairs are shriveled. If you make a braid, hang the finished braid upside down so the moisture drains out rather than back down into the onions.

Peas

◆107◆ **Pea basics, varieties.** All peas, both the shelling types and the edible-pod types, are early-spring vegetables. They need cool temperatures to germinate, and hot weather simply shuts the plants down. There are vine and bush varieties of both types, although most of the bush types are essentially short vines and many people grow them with some support.

Good varieties of shelling peas include Oregon Pioneer, Oregon Trail, and Olympia. For edible-pod peas, also called snow peas, the ones we associate with Chinese cooking, try Oregon Giant or Oregon Sugar Pod II. Sugar-snap peas, a third type, are relatively new. We have the prolific Dr. Baggett to thank for most of these fine varieties: Sugar Snap (the original), Sugar Ann, Snappy, Sugar Daddy, and Cascadia Snap; all do well in all parts of the Northwest, in cool weather.

108 Peas like soil on the sweet side. Most Northwest soils are naturally acidic, so you will probably have to add some lime (or wood ashes) to change the pH a bit. Do this a few days before planting; work it well into the soil.

109 Plant early in the year. For most gardeners, peas are the first thing that go in the ground. In the maritime areas of the Northwest, often you can put in your first group of seeds in January, and surely you want to have them in by President's Day.

Sometimes it's tricky to remember this, when the whole world seems locked into winter. But if your soil is not frozen, you can put in your peas. Remember, don't soak the seeds. They seem hard and tough, and you might be tempted, but resist. (See tip 66.)

110 **Watch for slugs and mildew.** The downside of planting extra-early in the spring is that often that is also the time when slugs are extra active. They just looooove the succulent seedlings when the peas first poke their heads out of the ground. One day you're admiring your beautiful babies, about to unfurl; the next day they're all gone. Be extra vigilant with your slug control. Or plant double, some for the slugs and some for you. Or start over; the new seedlings will quickly catch up.

Peas are susceptible to mildew. Because we grow them in cool weather, we also grow them in damp conditions, which promotes mildew. To counteract, don't water overhead, don't use sprays or sprinklers.

111 **If you live at the beach, you can grow peas in three seasons.** Most of the coastal areas in the Northwest have coolish weather through most of the summer, and you can plant a succession of peas to last from early spring through to fall.

112 **Give yourself a treat: become acquainted with sugar-snap peas.** Sugar-snap peas are, in my opinion, one of the Seven Wonders of the modern age; they are incredibly sweet and so crunchy that if you bend them in half, they snap (hence the name). The pods get fat, like shelling peas, but you eat the whole thing, pod and all. They are wonderful raw or cooked, but I'm betting you'll eat half your crop standing in the garden.

Their growing conditions are mostly like other peas, but they germinate better when the soil is a bit warmer; in cold, wet soil they often rot before they come up. This can present a tricky problem of timing: they germinate in warmer weather, grow best in cool weather.

To get around this, try Peter Chan's ingenious system. Start the seeds indoors (where you can control the temperature) in January, in small planting tubes made of rolled-up newspaper; the finished tube is bottomless, about 4 inches tall and 1 inch in diameter, tied together with string. When the seed has germinated, put the whole thing—newspaper and all—into the ground. Mr. Chan uses a bulb-planting tool to dig a perfectly round hole that is just the right diameter, and covers the entire package with soil, completely covering the leaves. The plant grows up through the soil cover, and the newspaper decomposes in place.

Peppers

⟨113⟩ **Pepper basics, varieties.** Both types of peppers—sweet and hot—are hot-season vegetables. The soil has to be warm, the air temperature hot, or they just won't grow. They need full sun, rich soil, regular fertilizing, and lots of water. Sweet peppers are green when young, then turn color as they mature. If the weather cooperates, leave them on the plant and you'll get glorious colors—red, yellow, orange, purple, creamy ivory, even chocolate brown—and much more vitamin content.

California Wonder (75 days from transplants) produces the classic squarish sweet bell pepper; this is the one you usually find in the supermarket, and it produces well in the home garden too. Gypsy (70 days) is a very strong hybrid and a vigorous producer. Even veggiephobic kids love chocolate peppers (color, not taste); Chocolate Beauty (75 days) is a nice one. Spend some time with seed catalogs, and you'll be amazed at the range of colors of the new varieties. If you think all bell peppers are green, you're in for a wonderful surprise.

For hot chili peppers, almost all varieties do well in the warmer parts of the Northwest (inland northern California and south central Oregon). In the Willamette Valley they also do well if you use black plastic to warm up the soil.

114 **Do everything in your power to accommodate the need for warmth.** Northwest summers can be very fickle, with several days of hot weather alternating with surprisingly cool temperatures. Cool nights, which are not uncommon in June, will cause plants to drop any blossoms they have formed. Obviously you can't control the weather (if you can, you don't need any advice from me) but there are things you can do to compensate.

For one thing, hold off as long as you can before putting these heat-loving plants into the garden. Start with sturdy, healthy transplants, as large as you can find. If you start your own seeds, choose varieties with the shortest maturity times; that way you can plant late and still have time for a full batch. Pay attention to the weather reports; if temperature drops are predicted, give the plants some protection. Surround plants with a bottomless black pot (see tip 22). Use plastic mulch around the plants to warm up the soil. Water them with solar-heated water (see tip 25). Rig up heat lamps (just kidding).

115 **Increase production with Epsom salts and fertilizer.** When blossoms appear, spray them with a light solution of Epsom salts in water. This helps to "set" the fruit. And peppers need consistent fertilizing while they are making fruit. Early in the season, when you first put them out, use fish emulsion and superphosphate. While the plants are actively growing and producing peppers, feed with a well-balanced fertilizer at least once a month.

⟨116⟩ Use matches to provide sulfur. Pepper plants need extra sulfur in the soil, and a nifty way to add it is with matches. Take a book of matches, tear off the cover, and put the bundle of matches in the bottom of the hole where you intend to plant the pepper. Cover the matches with 1 inch of soil, so the roots aren't burned by direct contact, then plant as usual. By the time the roots reach them, the matches will have dissolved out the sulfur into the soil.

⟨117⟩ You can force pepper plants to ripen the fruit at the end of the season. If it's obvious that cold weather is on the way and your plants still have immature peppers, you can encourage the ripening process by stressing the plants. Do this by pulling up slightly on the stem, or digging the ground close to the stem so as to cut through some of the side roots. Either way, this tears some of the feeder roots that the plant needs to keep growing and producing more flowers, and forces the plant instead to put its energy into ripening the fruit that is already set.

Potatoes

⟨118⟩ **Potato basics, varieties.** There was a time when I put potatoes in the category of "not worth bothering with because they're so cheap in the supermarket." No longer. Even standard varieties of potatoes taste much better fresh out of the garden. And if you grow your own you can experiment with the many new gourmet varieties that are soooo delicious and soooo expensive in the produce market.

Potato plants grow from so-called seed potatoes, which are not seeds in the true sense but small potatoes harvested specifically for the purpose. Think of the potatoes in the back of the cupboard that sprouted before you got a chance to use them, and you understand the process. Small seed potatoes can be planted whole; larger ones are cut into sections, with at least one "eye" each, preferably two. The new potatoes (your crop) form underground.

Important news on the potato front is the development of minitubers, from those geniuses at Oregon State University. These are very small seed potatoes (about as big as a walnut) that are grown in two stages: eyes from the potato are tissue cultured in a laboratory and then grown in a greenhouse under carefully controlled conditions. Minitubers harvested from these protected plants are free of the viruses that are so common to field-grown potatoes.

Almost all types of potatoes grow equally well in all parts of the Northwest, so your task here is to read catalogs carefully and choose from among the many temptations. If you think "potato" equals "white," you're in for a treat.

Among the gourmet types are those whose flesh is blue, yellow, purple, rosy pink, marbled red and yellow—all fun to try. Yukon Gold is very popular, and deservedly so: it's extra early (55 days), with a nice yellow color, pleasing texture, and such a rich, buttery taste that you don't need to add any butter. Red Pontiac is a favorite for red potatoes, a very vigorous producer. Fingerling potatoes (there are several varieties) are long and slender, so you can slice circles of consistent size for fancy potato salad. They have a moist, nonmealy texture and hold their shape when cut.

119 **Presprouting significantly speeds up the growing process.** About two weeks before it's time to plant the seed potatoes, bring them out from wherever you stored them when your catalog order arrived. Spread them one layer deep in a shallow box or nursery flat. Set the boxes in the main part of the house, where room temperatures are around 70 degrees and where they are exposed to medium amounts of sunlight, for about two weeks. The eyes on the potatoes will sprout into short, firm, sturdy stem sprouts.

If the seed potato is large, cut it into chunks with a sharp knife, taking care not to break off the sprouts. Otherwise, plant the whole thing. This presprouting process means you will have potatoes earlier and, many believe, more of them.

⟨120⟩ Three necessities for terrific potatoes are good soil, good soil, and good soil. Remember that your potatoes are growing underground. Rocky or heavy soil will produce twisted, stunted shapes. To get nicely shaped potatoes, and lots of them, you must have soil with a loose texture that allows room for the tubers to grow. Before planting, work in compost or other organic matter to make light, fluffy soil. (Or try any of the several growing techniques described just below.) If you can grow your potatoes in a raised bed, so much the better.

121 **Keep adding more soil to cover the stems as the plant grows.**
A potato plant produces tubers from nodules all along the stem, from the original seed piece to the soil surface. So, any technique that elongates that distance will provide you with more potatoes. The basic way of planting potatoes is called hilling: you dig a hole about 8 inches deep, put in the seed piece, cover with dirt up to about 4 inches. As the plant grows, continue mounding up soil around the stem, leaving just a few inches of foliage uncovered; you can't see them, but little potatoes are growing from the buried stem.

There are several alternate ways to accomplish the same thing. One is to plant the seed in a shallow trench, then cover with a thin layer of soil and a thick layer (6 inches or more) of organic mulch. Hay or straw is best; leaves or grass clippings will also work. As the plant grows, continue to add on more mulch. When the potatoes are ready to harvest, just reach into the straw and collect them. This is a good method to use if your soil is not so great: heavy clay, rocky, or very shallow.

Another alternate uses old automobile tires. Lay one tire flat on the ground, plant a seed potato in a shallow depression, fill in with good-quality soil. As the plant grows up above the level of the tire, add a second tire and more soil (or mulch), and then a third, and so on. At harvest time, remove the tires and you have a cylindrical hill full of potatoes.

Still another way: use a barrel, a round cage made of mesh wire, or a wooden box. Same technique: plant the seed potato, keep adding soil or straw as the plant grows, covering up all but the top few inches of the leaves. Just make sure, in all cases, that the growing tubers are not exposed to light, or the skins turn green, which is the sign for presence of a toxin.

122 Water consistently while the plants are growing. This is one of the secrets for even, perfectly formed potatoes. From the time the leaves first show themselves until you think tubers are formed, keep the soil evenly and consistently moist. Once the potatoes are nearly ready to be harvested, cut down on the water; it's much easier to dig them from dry ground.

123 Potatoes are ready to harvest when the plants begin to flower. This is a general guideline that doesn't always apply (there are some varieties of potato that don't form flowers) but it works well as a rule of thumb. If you're not sure, dig down with your fingers; can you feel potatoes next to the stem? Many people prefer to use a spading fork instead of a shovel, thinking it damages fewer tubers. If your soil is really loose or you used one of the straw methods, you can just dig them out with your hands.

◆124◆ Don't grow potatoes in the same spot two years in a row. It's call rotation, and it's a good idea for all plants but really essential with potatoes. One of the unfortunate facts of life is that potatoes are subject to more serious problems with voracious insects and disease than most other vegetables are, and they stay in the nearby ground after the potatoes have been harvested.

Radishes

◆125◆ Radish basics, varieties. Growing radishes is a snap. They mature fast (less than a month from planting to eating) and have few problems. They're nice for northwesterners because they do much better in cool weather. About the only thing you need to be aware of is making sure they have lots of water; they turn pithy and bitter if grown in dry soil. Radishes are a great way to introduce children to vegetable gardening, because they grow so fast they keep up with kids' attention span.

Among the familiar round red radishes, two classics are Champion (28 days) and Cherry Belle (25 days). Children are captivated by Easter Egg (25 days), which produces round radishes in several different shades: red, rose, purple, and white. White Icicle (27 days) and French Breakfast (25 days) are finger shaped, about 2 inches long. Daikon (oriental) radishes are much larger and take much longer to reach maturity (60 to 70 days). Like other radishes, they don't grow as well in hot weather, so timing these can be tricky. Best used as a fall crop, for they hold up well under cold temperatures.

126 **Use radishes as row markers and soil conditioners.** Radishes germinate amazingly fast, and grow fast too. You can use this trait to advantage with other seeds that are very slow to germinate (like carrots). Mix the two together and plant the mixture. Radishes will break through the soil fast, showing you where your seeds are and keeping the surface of the soil from becoming hard and crusty. By the time they're ready to harvest, the carrots (or whatever) should be coming on.

127 **Radishes will bolt in hot weather.** Usually this can be avoided, because radishes are ready to eat in such a short time you'll pull them up before the plant bolts. But if this does happen, all is not lost. Let the plant flower and set seed, then gather the seedpods while they're still green. Add them to salads for a tangy crunch, to stir-fry dishes, or to any pickles you're making.

Spinach

128 **Spinach basics, varieties.** Spinach is happy in cool weather, and relatively fast growing, which means that northwesterners can usually get two full crops: spring and fall. For best results, keep it growing fast with lots of water and nitrogen-rich fertilizer. You want to get your spring crop to reach maturity before hot weather settles in, for otherwise spinach is subject to bolting just like lettuce.

Some of the oldie-but-goodie standard varieties are Tyee, Olympia, and Long-Standing Bloomsdale (all around 45 days).

129 **For spinach in summer, get acquainted with New Zealand spinach.** Botanically, it's not really spinach, but the taste is very similar. The leaves are fleshy and crisp, and the plant is not bothered by hot weather. The trade-off is that it's much longer to maturity (70 days) and extremely slow to germinate. Many spinach lovers plant regular spinach and New Zealand spinach at the same time—early spring—for a continuous harvest of vitamin-rich greens right through the summer.

◆130◆ **Plant in summer for a fall and winter crop.** Spinach is another of those wonderful vegetables that northwesterners can grow in our mild winters, but there's one small problem: the seeds don't germinate well when the weather is hot, which it often is when you'd be planting your second crop. To get around this, first soak your seed overnight and then put them in the refrigerator for a few days, then plant as usual. You can be going out in the garden for fresh spinach in December, something not possible in many parts of the country.

Squash and Pumpkins

◆131◆ **Squash basics, varieties.** There are two broad groups of squash: summer and winter. Summer squash are small (relatively), thin-skinned, and fast producers; this group includes zucchini, crookneck, and those cute little scalloped rounds. Winter squash are larger and have dense flesh and a hard skin that retards spoilage, so they can be stored in a dry area through the winter (hence the name). Familiar winter squash are acorn, hubbard, butternut, and pumpkins. All need hot weather, lots of water, and a very rich soil; in return they make lots of squashes hiding under lots of large lush foliage. Squash plants take up a *lot* of room; plan accordingly.

All kinds of summer squash do well in all areas of the Pacific Northwest, except the very short-season areas along the coast or high elevations. There are vine and bush versions of practically all types; read the seed packet carefully. Seneca zucchini (42 days) is unusual in that it grows well even in cool summer. In addition to the familiar long green cylinder, some zucchinis have yellow skin (one is Gold Rush, 50 days) and some are green and round (45 days). Supersett (50 days) and Sundance (50 days) are both excellent yellow crooknecks. The round squashes with the scalloped edges are collectively called pattypans (the name of one of the original varieties); Sunburst (50 days) makes yellow fruit, Peter Pan (50 days) makes green, and White (47 days) produces fruit that is a pale greenish-white.

You may hear old-time gardeners claim that hubbard has the best flavor of any winter squash, and that may be so, but the truth is it's just too big a plant for most home gardens. Fortunately, much of the sweet, rich flavor has been captured in several new breeds: Delicata (one variety is Sugar Loaf, 100 days, developed by Dr. Baggett), butternut (try Ponca or Waltham, both 90 days), and Buttercup (Sweet Emerald, a bush variety, takes 85 days). For acorn squash (also collectively called Danish squash) choose Table King, Table Queen, or Table Ace; all mature in 85 days or less, which means you can get a harvest even where the season is too short for other winter squash.

For pumpkins, unless you have lots of space and growing time, look for varieties that produce "mini" pumpkins (like Jack Be Little, 90 days, or Baby Boo, 85 days).

132 Keep large winter squash off the ground. If your plants are the vining type, squashes lying directly on the ground are susceptible to disease and to rot where water pools under them. If possible, support them in a sling made from panty hose, tying it to a nearby fence. This also provides more air circulation. Or set each squash on an empty tuna can.

133 Watch for mildew in late summer. It's quite common on squash and cucumber plants in western Oregon and Washington. Here's a good home remedy: make a solution of 2 teaspoons baking soda and ½ teaspoon liquid dishwashing detergent in a gallon of water. Put it in a spray bottle and spray all over the leaves as soon as you see the first sign of mildew.

134 **Know when to harvest.** Winter squash are ready when the skin is so tough you can't get your fingernail into it, and when the part that sits on the ground is no longer white but has turned yellow. Cut off with a sharp knife and leave an inch or two of stem attached to the squash; that will keep it from rotting at the stem end while it's in storage. Keep in a cool room, around 60°F.

Summer squash are ready whenever you are. One of the joys of having squash in your garden is you can collect them when they are tiny, still with blossom attached, for a super elegant treat like in the fanciest restaurants. Of course you may prefer to let them get to a more normal size, but don't overdo it. They are best when small and tender. And if one gets away from you (zucchini always seems to do that), cut it off even if you don't plan to eat it; if you leave it, the plant will soon stop producing.

135 **Eat late-season winter squash fresh.** It always happens: the cool days of autumn arrive before all your winter squash have developed the hard skin that is necessary for winter storage. Out at the end of the vine, the part that is actively growing, are some small, immature squash that will never reach full size before frost. Don't let them go to waste; snip them off and cook like summer squash.

Tomatoes

136 **Tomato basics, varieties.** If you do nothing else, at least put in one tomato plant; there's just nothing like that luscious, sensuous, sun-warmed taste. Unfortunately, tomatoes are hot-weather vegetables, and growing them is a challenge in short-season areas of the Northwest. Even in valley areas west of the Cascades, many years are iffy. Dedicated gardeners turn growing tomatoes into a competitive sport, racing one another to see who gets the first red fruit. To counteract uncooperative weather, pull out all the stops for warming up the tomato bed (see Beating the Odds: Spring).

Tomatoes are grouped into two large categories by growth habit. Determinate plants grow to a certain predetermined size and then no taller. Indeterminate plants grow and grow and grow, in a lanky, flamboyant way, until frost stops them. In a good year (good meaning warm) just two or three indeterminate plants can turn your tomato patch into a jungle while your back is turned. Determinate plants are sturdy and stocky and tend to produce their tomatoes in a concentrated period; indeterminates keep on producing till frost. If you buy tomato plants at the garden center, they aren't always marked with this information. Either buy seeds from a catalog that includes full information, or study a good catalog to learn which varieties are which before you head for the garden center.

Tomatoes are also grouped by type: slicing and eating tomatoes (medium to large size); plum tomatoes (also generically called Roma), which are oval and very dense, the best for making sauce because they have much more flesh than juice; and cherry tomatoes, anywhere from the size of a large pea to a ping-pong ball. All northwesterners should have at least one cherry tomato plant. Because they're so small, individual tomatoes mature faster; even in the worst green-tomato years, you'll get some ripe ones.

Oregon Spring (yet another of Dr. Baggett's miracles) is the best news northwesterners have had in some time; this compact determinate plant tolerates cool weather and produces large, delicious tomatoes in a short period (58 days). [All dates are from time of transplanting.] If you live at the beach or in the mountains (or anywhere in the Northwest when we have a cool summer), this is the one for you.

Other varieties recommended for short-season areas include Santiam (determinate, 55 days), Early Cascade (indeterminate, 63 days), and Early Girl (indeterminate, 62 days). Champion (indeterminate) and Celebrity (determinate) both are ready in about 70 days, both delicious. The excellent Oregon Star (determinate, 58 days, also from Dr. Baggett) is somewhat plum-shaped.

Among the cherry tomatoes, you won't find anything more popular than Sweet 100, unless it's Sweet 100 Plus (indeterminate, 70 days), a newer variety that resists cracking. Yellow pear tomatoes (indeterminate, 70 days) are pretty, and kids love them. Golden Nugget (determinate, 60 days, Dr. Baggett again) is a small plant but produces a lusty crop of golfball-size yellow fruit.

<137> **Get a long tomato season by using different varieties.** In April, start seeds indoors of an early, cold-tolerant type like Oregon Spring. If it's a determinate plant, you can grow it in a container, which you can position in your warmest spot. Add plastic covering when the temperature falls.

Then a couple of weeks later, start seeds of an indeterminate kind; in late May or early June, plant them in the garden and often you'll still be picking tomatoes in October.

⟨138⟩ Plant tomatoes deeply. The stem should be completely buried, all the way to the first leaves. Roots will form all along the stem, to help the plant take in water. And if you should find yourself with an especially leggy plant (an orphan at the garden center, or your own windowsill baby that got out of hand), dig a trench and lay the plant in the ground sideways. End with a little mound of dirt and gently bend the leafy part upward. Roots will form all along the buried stem. Mound up the soil in a circle a few inches from the plant, so that you create a sort of moat around it. When you irrigate, fill up that moat with water.

⟨139⟩ Use plastic to protect young plants. If you live in a high-elevation area (or if it's just one of the cold years that we seem to have in the Northwest), you have to put your tomatoes in the ground while the weather is still cool or you don't have a prayer of getting ripe tomatoes before frost comes. The way to get around this is to give the baby plants lots of protection in the cool spring.

Lots of gardeners in eastern Idaho and Montana depend on a commercial product called Walls-o-Water, which consists of two concentric circles of stiff fluted plastic; when the inner space is filled with water, it collects and holds solar heat. But you can accomplish much the same thing with rigid sheet plastic shaped into a cone and pushed into the ground around the baby; leave an opening at the top for air circulation. Even simpler and less expensive: take one of those cone-shaped tomato cages, turn it upside down over the young plant, and cover it with a plastic bag from the dry cleaners. You've created a mini-greenhouse.

140 **Consistent watering is important, especially once fruit starts to form.** Alternating periods of wet and dry are responsible for misshapen fruit and sometimes for rot. Very heavy rains over a short period can cause the tomatoes to take in so much water the skins burst. You can't control the rain, but you can be careful with irrigating.

141 **Add a bit of lime to the soil around tomato plants; and add eggshells for calcium.** If your soil is acidic (which it is, if you live west of the Cascades) a handful of dolomite lime worked into the soil at planting time is very beneficial for tomatoes. Before you plant your tomatoes, bury a handful of finely crushed eggshells in the hole and cover lightly with soil. They are a fine (and free) source of calcium, which helps prevent blossom end rot. Tomatoes need very little fertilizing; a side dressing once a year is usually enough. And make sure it is low in nitrogen; you're not growing tomatoes for the foliage.

142 **Prune judiciously.** Tomato plants benefit from careful pruning. When the plant is young, prune down to three main stems: the central stem and two very sturdy side branches. This gives good air circulation near the base of the plant. You can let secondary branches form on these three main stems, and that will give you all the tomatoes you need.

As the plant grows, remove all axial branches that have leaves but no flowers; they just take energy that the plant needs for making fruit, and the plants need good air circulation. Do *not*, however, get carried away and take off all the leaves. If you have indeterminate plants, you may want to cut off the main stem when it reaches 4 or 5 feet; otherwise it just keeps growing taller.

For all types, at the end of summer prune off all branches that have only leaves and flowers; there isn't going to be time for those flowers to develop into fruit, and the plant needs all its energy to go into ripening tomatoes. About mid-September, prune off everything but branches with fruit that is already turning color.

143 **Stakes or cages?** You can grow tomatoes without any kind of support, letting them sprawl on the ground every which way, but you'll regret it. Fruit that touches the ground is an easy target for insects and disease, rots in contact with damp soil, and is almost impossible not to step on.

Tomato cages are inexpensive and at first seem to be an easy solution. But the common type of commercial product is too short to do any good for anything except patio-size plants. Many people think cages tend to promote leaf growth, at the expense of fruits, and also encourage white fly infestations.

A much better alternative is a tall circle of heavy wire with a grid wide enough to get your hands in, such as the stuff contractors use to reinforce concrete. Wrap the sides in plastic, and you can put your tomatoes in the ground two or three weeks earlier than normal.

Sturdy stakes are another good way to go; they're easy to work with, easy to move, easy to store. Put the first one in the ground the same day you put in the tomato plant. After you train two main side branches (see tip 142), add two more stakes nearby. I use a variation on berry trellises: five short metal posts set in a W outline, strung with three strands of medium-gauge wire. I plant the small plants in the notches of the W, and tie the branches loosely to the wires as the plants grow.

Turnips and Friends

144 **Turnip basics, varieties.** Turnips, rutabagas, and parsnips may not be as popular root crops as carrots and radishes, but they are worth knowing about. All grow well in cool weather and poorly in hot weather, which earns them a place on the "perfect for the Northwest" list. Plant very early in spring for an early summer crop, in late summer for a fall crop. Most varieties will survive the first winter frost, and with mulching will overwinter completely.

The roots (the part you eat) are good raw as well as cooked, and young turnip greens (the leaves) have a tangy flavor that many people are fond of. Mature turnips and rutabagas can be dug and stored through the winter. All these root vegetables need well-prepared soil beds; in heavy or rocky soil, their growth is stunted.

Purple-top White Globe is the standard, familiar turnip, reaching a 3-inch size in 55 days. Turnips are very popular in Japan, and many nice Japanese varieties are available to us; Tokyo Cross (35 days) and Market Express (30 days) both make small, tender-crisp turnips. Shogoin (60 days) is the best for turnip greens. For rutabagas, try American Purple Top or Purple-Top Yellow (both 90 days). For parsnips Hollow Crown (105 days) is good.

145 Grow kohlrabi instead. The biggest challenge with long-growing root crops is that they are often attacked by root maggots before they are ready to dig up. Unless people in your family really admire the taste of turnips, you may decide it's too much trouble. A nifty alternative: grow kohlrabi. This oriental vegetable is actually a member of the cabbage family. The base of the stem forms into a round bulb the size of a softball, with leaves growing from around the sides. The softball is the part you eat; it's crunchy like a turnip but milder and sweeter. It's great in salads or stir-fry dishes, or steamed as a side dish. Because the bulb is aboveground, root maggots don't bother it. And besides, the plant is awfully cute.

To grow kohlrabi, remember that it's a cabbage cousin. Plant seeds directly in the ground in early spring or late summer. In hot weather the bulb may not form at all, or turns woody. The most commonly available varieties are Early White Vienna (55 days), which has green skin and white flesh, and Early Purple Vienna (60 days) with purple skin. Grand Duke (50 days), a hybrid green, is superior.

Herbs and Flowers

146 **Grow herbs and flowers in among your vegetables.** They attract honeybees, help control damaging insects, boost the flavor of your vegetable dishes, and nourish the soul. Lemon balm is famous for its ability to attract bees, and you need honeybees in your garden to pollinate the flowers on the cucumbers, squashes, and melons. Other bee-attracting herbs: bee balm (bergamot), lavender, sage (when it blooms), hyssop, borage—in fact, anything with a fragrant flower. Extra benefit for humans: flowers of herb plants are edible too, and make gorgeous garnishes.

Hyssop is a multipurpose wonderplant. This perennial herb is easy to grow and fills several functions in your garden. It flowers all summer and well into the fall, and the flowers attract both bees and butterflies. It is also said that hyssop repels the cabbage moth that does such damage to cabbage, broccoli, cauliflower, and their cousins. Cynics may put that in the category of old wives' tales, but the truth is, those old wives have often been right.

147 **Flowers of many herbs attract beneficial insects.** The group of plants that produces a flower cluster shaped like an upside-down umbrella (think of a dill plant) is called the umbelliferae. Many of the plants in this group are among our culinary herbs: dill, anise, parsley, cilantro, sweet cicely, caraway, and fennel. These umbrella flowers are favorites of very small wasps that you will be glad to have around, for they feed on the eggs and larvae of insects that do bad things in your garden. When you see a swarm of tiny black or green insects around the flowers of your herbs, say thank you and leave them in peace.

148 **Use flowers to help control harmful insects.** Marigolds seem to repel the nematodes that attack root vegetables. Nasturtiums are said to help control cabbage moths. Nasturtiums also are often used as a "trap plant" for aphids, which seem to go crazy over them. If you use nasturtiums this way, think carefully about positioning. The plant keeps aphids away from susceptible vegetables by drawing them to itself, like a magnet. But if you plant nasturtiums very near a tempting vegetable, the aphids will travel over.

Nasturtium flowers, leaves, and buds are also edible, and make a knockout addition to a green salad; just make sure you check for aphids first.

149 **Grow a few sunflowers.** The cheerful flowers will boost your morale on even the gloomiest days, and the nutritious seeds make a healthful snack, provided the birds don't beat you to them. Or consider leaving them on the plant for the birds to enjoy. They will repay you by eating a few bugs that you'd just as soon not have around. Plant pole beans and sunflowers together, and the beans will climb right up the sunflower stalk. When the sunflowers are about a foot high, plant bean seeds right next to them.

DEALING WITH THE INEVITABLE

❧ ❧ ❧

Weeds

150 Do your weeding right after it rains. They come up much easier when the soil is wet. Don't wait for a warm, sunny day; by the time that happens, the weeds will have gotten away from you. It's one more aspect of the good news/bad news scenario of gardening in the Pacific Northwest. Working outside when it's drizzling may be hard on your spirits, but on the other hand it's very satisfying to rip those little devils out, and that goes a long way toward making up for getting your hair wet and your hands muddy.

151 **Get rid of weeds before they set seed.** Seeds from some types of weeds remain in the soil for 20 years. You can't do much about correcting someone else's past sloppiness, but be sure not to perpetuate it. Be especially vigilant in February and March. You can put the corpses on the vegetable beds as mulch, unless they have seeds.

And be sure to weed all around the garden, not just in it. Weed seeds travel. Even worse, weeds and tall grasses harbor diseases and damaging insects through the winter; they lie in wait for more hospitable conditions—like your vegetable bed at its peak.

152 **Make a newspaper weed barrier between rows.** Spread several layers of newspaper between rows in the garden. Cover the newspaper with organic material: grass clippings, yard debris (run the lawn mower over it to chop it up), straw, pine needles, whatever. This will effectively hold down weeds through the summer. In fall and winter, the newspaper will gradually break down and both it and the stuff on top will enrich the soil.

Slugs

153 **First defense is prevention: keep the area clean.** Don't let the area near the garden get overgrown, and don't pile up debris; this provides the kind of environment that slugs love. But hold on, you may ask, what about the other suggestions about heavy mulch around the vegetable plants; isn't that Slug Heaven too? Yes it is, but in all probability you'll be using mulch during the hot months and slugs aren't as much of a problem then. The time you need to be careful is fall, when you're cleaning up the garden at the end of the season.

154 **Second defense is hunt for eggs.** Slugs lay eggs in clusters that look like tapioca pudding but transparent. The clusters are about an inch below the soil. In likely areas, turn the soil over frequently. If you expose an egg cluster, scoop it up and put it into a pan of salty water.

155 **Anything with a scratchy texture will repel slugs.** With their soft bodies, they don't like to travel over sharp, scratchy surfaces. Any of these materials spread around a plant will deter slugs: coarse sand, kitty litter, diatomaceous earth, roughly crushed eggshells. The problem is, these materials work only when they're dry, so when it rains you'll have to put down new stuff every day. Unfortunately, the rainy periods are also the worst slug times.

156 **Slug bait works just fine, but use it with care.** The bait is poisonous, and it is as attractive to cats and dogs as it is to slugs, so you need to be careful how you use it. Also, it needs to be kept dry. Peter Chan's margarine tub trick accomplishes both.

Cut out a square hole, about one inch square, about halfway up one side of a 1-pound margarine container. Bury the container so that the bottom of the "doorway" is level with the soil. That way the slugs can crawl in but your pets can't easily knock it over. Fill with a layer of bait, and put the top on. The top keeps the rain off and provides additional protection for curious animals. But remember: put the traps at the outer edges of the garden, not inside near the plants. You don't want to attract slugs into the middle of your garden, munching all the way.

An organic alternative to this technique is to put melon rinds or lettuce bits in the container instead of bait. Check each morning, and dump your catch down the toilet.

157 **Trap slugs by setting out objects they like to cling to**. You have probably noticed every time you pick up a small board, rock, nursery tray, or any other reasonably flat surface, that a whole bunch of slugs are having a party on the bottom. Turn that trait to your advantage. Deliberately set out things that slugs like, such as small boards, shingles, even thick pads of newspaper. Early the next morning, scrape the nasty little things into a container that has some slug bait, ammonia, or dishwashing detergent in it. Or, if you can stand it, snip each one in half with scissors or your pruners.

Empty pots turned upside down are also good traps, but leave some openings for the slugs to crawl inside. Either prop one edge on a stick, or choose an old pot that has a big chip out of the rim.

<158> **Ammonia kills slugs.** Make a mixture about one part ammonia to three parts water and fill a spray bottle. Keep the bottle in your gardening tool bucket, and be ready to spritz a slug whenever you see one. In the daytime you won't see as many, but when you do, show no mercy.

Bugs Friendly and Otherwise

<159> **Learn to distinguish between good bugs and bad.** Bees and wasps pollinate the flowers of vegetable plants. Wasps eat many kinds of harmful insects. Ladybugs and lacewings feed

on aphids. Spiders help control the population of insects that damage plants. Ground beetles, millipedes, sow bugs, and earthworms play a vital role in soil quality, by helping organic materials break down or providing aeration or both. Take the time to learn the good guys; many garden centers have a bug identifier chart or book.

160 **Attract birds to the garden; raise chickens if you can.** Many species of birds are natural bug-busters. Chickadees eat their weight in worms and bugs every day. Attract them with sunflower seeds, either *au naturel* or in a feeder. Leaf rollers are difficult for humans to deal with, because sprays and dusts have a hard time penetrating the rolled-up leaf, but orioles can get right in there with their beaks and snatch the bugs out. Nail orange halves onto your garden fence posts to attract orioles.

To bring all kinds of birds to your garden, give them special shelter. Save your old Christmas tree, and prop it up somewhere in or near the garden area. Decorate it with popcorn balls, suet, pieces of fruit, and fruit rinds.

If local ordinances permit, keep a few chickens and let them roam in the garden. They'll eat up cutworms, beetles, larvae, insect eggs, and weeds, and leave you some very nice fertilizer in return.

Their scratching also loosens the soil. You may want to set up temporary, portable fences around vegetable beds, to keep the chickens in place while they do their thing, then move them to the next bed.

161 **Invite toads and frogs to move in; they eat a lot of bugs.** A clay pot with a big notch chipped out of one side, upside down, makes a nice welcoming toad house. It should be fairly large. This is a good thing to do with damaged pots you can't otherwise use.

162 **Floating row covers keep out many types of harmful insects.** These row covers are made of very lightweight fabric that lets water and sunlight through but not critters. You bury the edges in the soil, leaving lots of slack. Because the fabric "floats," the plants push it up as they grow. But because the plants are completely encased, flying and crawling insects have no way in. This is a very effective barrier to cabbage moths, white fly, cutworms, leaf miners, and root maggots. An added bonus, very valuable in the Northwest: the covers also warm the soil in spring and provide a light shade in summer.

◆**163** **Finely sifted wood ashes are an organic substitute for insecticide dust.** On tomatoes, potatoes, beans, squash, and cucumbers, ashes help with aphids and flea beetles. Also effective against aphids and cabbage loopers on the cabbage family: cauliflower, broccoli, Brussels sprouts, etc. Pick up an old flour sifter at the thrift store just for this purpose and store it with your garden tools. And don't buy a special implement for applying the dust. Put the fine ashes in an old detergent bottle with a squirt top and squirt them right on the plants.

◆**164** **Insecticides can be made from detergent and ammonia.** In garden centers you can buy so-called insecticidal soap, but you can make your own substitute. A weak solution of dishwashing detergent plus baking soda in a spray bottle works well against aphids and some other insects too. If you have real soap (i.e., Ivory, White King, Fels Naptha) that's better, although many people use whatever detergent they have on hand and report good results.

Ammonia mixed with water in a spray bottle is another good way to go; use about one-third ammonia to two-thirds water. Keep a spray bottle with you when you walk through the garden, ready to zap the bad guys.

165 **Trap earwigs with newspaper or oil.** Roll up sections of newspaper and scatter them throughout the garden. During the night, earwigs will crawl in. The next morning, unroll and shake them out into a large can with a cover, like a 3-pound coffee can, with a layer of oil in the bottom; whenever you're ready, dispose of the goop in the garbage. This large can is a good dumping ground for all kinds of harmful bugs, not just the earwigs.

Another technique that works well with earwigs is to set out tuna cans or pie plates with a layer of oil in the bottom; the earwigs are attracted to the oil and drown in it because they are unable to crawl out.

166 **For root maggots, use Epsom salts on the ground and put barriers around seedlings.** These tiny worms can do a lot of damage to root crops, and you won't know it until you dig up your radishes or turnips to eat them. You can apply insecticide at time of planting, or use Epsom salts as an organic alternative. Put the salts in shallow depressions and plant the seeds right on top.

Root maggots are also attracted to members of the cabbage family, and will attack the stems right at the soil level. Before you know it, your pretty little plants will just keel over. Protect young plants with a physical barrier, such as a collar made of heavy paper. Be sure and push it part way down into the soil, so the maggots can't get to the plant from underground. The cardboard cores from bathroom tissue work well for this; they're the right size and they're nice and stiff. You can also use tin cans with top and bottom cut out, or empty orange juice containers. Any of these collars will also protect against cutworms, which will slice your seedlings right off at the soil line.

167 **Grow some plants as sacrifices to control aphids.** Nasturtiums are a good choice. But grow these trap plants far away from the vegetables, so the aphids can't travel over so easily. Many aphids have wings, and will simply fly to new food sources when they get good and ready. Check the undersides of the leaves. When one has a good cluster of aphids, pick it off and destroy it. Or squash the little suckers with your fingers; gloves help.

168 **Spray aphids with the garden hose.** Another organic, nontoxic way to get rid of aphids is to spray the affected part of the plant *hard* with a garden hose. Get close to the plant and adjust the hose nozzle to a tight stream. The idea is not to drown the aphids but to physically knock them off. When the weather is really warm—late July and August—you'll have to do this every few days. Don't try this on young seedlings; the hard blast of water will destroy a tiny plant. Also effective against aphids are dusting with wood ashes (tip 163) and spraying with either an ammonia solution or a detergent solution (tip 164).

169 **Leaf miners are a problem with vegetables we grow for their leaves.** Spinach, lettuce, and other leafy crops can be ruined by "tunnels" all over the foliage. Floating row covers will help keep the adult leaf miners out, and plastic mulch will keep them from laying eggs in the soil.

170 **Develop an ecosystem mindset.** When you grow, harvest, and eat vegetables, you are participating in a natural process. Along the way, some bugs will do some damage to some plants; this is inevitable. Rather than panicking and rushing to the insecticides at the first sign of trouble, pause and consider: Just how much damage are you likely to sustain, and is that sufficient justification for putting poisonous chemicals in the soil and the atmosphere or for creating a murderous spirit within yourself? Do you even know what is causing the problem?

Keep your perspective; even if you lose your whole first set of seedlings, it's not the end of the world—it's just cabbage. Replant. Do the best you can, and don't let these nuisances rob you of the joy of gardening.

Plant Diseases and Other Problems

171 **The dampness of the maritime Northwest climate causes several fungal diseases; powdery mildew is very common.** West of the Cascades, the pathogens that cause these diseases are around all the time. When the weather is both damp and warm, they really kick in and can easily overwhelm your garden. Mildew is the most prevalent, and it is particularly common on pole beans, squash, and cucumbers in mid to late summer.

Your best defense is prevention. The most important factor for all fungi is adequate air circulation. When you plant, allow plenty of space between plants, and prune away excess foliage as the plants grow. Do your watering in the morning, so leaves have a chance to dry off during the day.

When you see the first signs of mildew, cut off and completely dispose of the affected leaves. Then spray the plant every few days, either with a chemical fungicide or this homemade remedy: 2 teaspoons of baking soda and ½ teaspoon liquid dish detergent mixed into a gallon of water.

⟨172⟩ Crop rotation will avert many problems. Eggs from plant-specific insects, plant viruses, and harmful bacteria often tend to stay in one spot. If next year you plant the same things in the same spot, you are just helping them flourish for another season. If you rotate plants each year, you may avoid many of the problems. This is mandatory for potatoes and very important for tomatoes, which are subject to diseases that persist in the soil, and a good idea for everything else.

⟨173⟩ Strawberry baskets will protect young seedlings from birds. Overall, birds are very good to have around, but when they take a fancy to your newly sprouted seedlings you are allowed to get annoyed. They seem to go for the very first leaves of beans, cucumbers, and melons, leaving only a bare stump that will probably die. When the seeds first push through the soil, cover each with one of those green plastic strawberry baskets you've been saving because they're too good to throw away. By the time the seedling is pushing against the top of the basket, there's enough foliage that a bird nibble won't be fatal.

174 Citrus peels scattered around the garden will keep cats away. Even the most passionate cat lovers don't want their pets using the vegetable beds for a litter box. It smells, it's nasty to work around, and it can be dangerous: cat poop often carries disease-causing bacteria. If you have enough room, you can do even better by planting a separate "cat garden." Keep the soil nice and fluffy, plant catnip, set out some drinking water. The cats will gravitate to this area and leave your vegetables alone.

175 Hang bags of dog hair around the garden to discourage small animals. Raccoons, possums, rabbits, even deer will not want to come too close when they smell dog. Save the dog hair when you groom Fido, and hang small bundles in net bags at various spots around the garden. If you don't have a dog of your own, offer to do it for a neighbor. Or make friends with the proprietor of a dog-grooming parlor.

176 Blood meal helps keep deer away. Throughout the Northwest, deer present serious problems to gardeners; they'll graze their way right through everything you have planted. Fences work, as long as they are 7 or 8 feet high; you'd be surprised how high a small deer can jump.

Another deterrent that will appeal to vegetable gardeners is blood meal, a soil amendment sold in large bags in garden centers. Take several squares of fabric (like old bandannas) and tie about a cupful of blood meal into each one; hang them around the garden. Every month or so, empty the bag into the garden soil and replace with fresh contents.

YEAR-ROUND SUCCESS

🌿 🌿 🌿

Containers

⟨177⟩ **Growing vegetables in containers solves lots of problems.** If your soil is heavy clay (which it is, if you live west of the Cascades) and you don't have the energy to prepare an entire garden area, or if you live in high desert areas with sandy soil that is inhospitable to plants, you can still have fresh produce by bringing in potting soil and growing vegetables in containers.

Because the working area is so much smaller, both spring planting and winter cleanup are a lot easier. If your containers are on display in public areas (balcony, deck, patio) you will probably have a tendency to hover over them, and so are more likely to spot any problems more quickly. Besides, if you live in an apartment or on a Puget Sound houseboat, you just plain don't have any other choice.

178 **Keep large containers on rollers so you can move them.** One of the chief advantages of having vegetables in pots is that they're portable. You can move them to the sunniest spot in spring and fall and to shade (if that's what you need) in summer. To make this possible, either buy or build small platforms with rollers. Put the container in place before you even start filling it; when full of potting soil, it's too heavy to lift.

179 **Use plants that stay relatively small.** You have an amazing selection of vegetables to choose from. Beets, carrots, turnips—all the root crops are especially well suited to containers because they love the loose soil. The leafy vegetables are a good workable size and very beautiful besides: red or white Swiss chard, the dark green ruffly leaves of spinach or kale, lettuce with leaves in red, bronze, and all shades of green. There are container-size varieties of tomatoes; anything with "midget" or "dwarf" or "patio" in the name is a good bet. Pepper plants are perfect for pots. Herbs are a natural for containers, and so are scallions.

If you have some really big containers you could probably manage bush varieties of squash and cucumbers. You can even, if you are determined, grow pole beans or peas; either insert a trellis or position the container next to a wall and run strings from the pot to a windowsill. Bush beans are small enough in size, but you probably won't get enough produce from one container's worth of bushes to make it worthwhile.

◇180◇ **Don't overlook hanging containers.** Multiply your patio gardening space by growing vegetables in hanging baskets. It is even more critical to pay attention to watering, because most hanging containers are smaller than floor-standing ones due to weight concerns. Think in terms of drooping down rather than vining up: cherry tomatoes, peas, cucumbers. New Zealand spinach works nicely.

◇181◇ **Watch your watering.** Soil in containers (especially clay ones) dries out faster than an equivalent area in the ground, especially when the weather is both hot and windy. Be prepared to water often, perhaps every day in the dead of summer. Put lots of peat moss in the potting mix; it holds water well.

Also be careful of really hot weather. On the dry side of the mountains, and even west of the Cascades in July and August, a string of very hot days can cook the roots of plants in containers, particularly if you're using black plastic pots. Give them an insulation layer as protection by setting them down inside larger pots and filling in the space with coarse bark chips.

Raised Beds

⟨182⟩ **Raised beds belong in every Northwest garden.** The benefits are many: By virtue of being higher than the surrounding area, they automatically provide improved drainage, very important in areas with clay soil, which is to say, everywhere west of the Cascades. They also are warmer than flat ground, and that is very helpful in areas where spring and even early summer can stay cool—which, again, is most of the Northwest. Even just a few degrees makes a big difference.

Raised beds allow you to grow intensively, so you need less fertilizer, less mulch, and less water. And because they are a contained area, chores are easier to manage. If you need to bring in compost, manure, sand, topsoil, or whatever, you can work one bed at a time and not feel overwhelmed.

Just remember: once you make your bed, don't walk on it. Make it narrow, so that you can reach into the middle from the paths (3 feet is good). If you never step on the soil in the raised bed, it never gets compacted.

183 **To frame or not to frame?** When planning raised beds, you have a choice of construction technique. You can build up mounds by shoveling only, digging out paths and piling the extra onto the mounds. This is easier and involves less expense, and in the drier areas of the Northwest will work fine. But in areas where it rains steadily, eventually the rain will break these beds down, and you'll have to start over. So west of the mountains, you're better off in the long run to build a supporting frame of lumber.

Some outdoor lumber is treated with a moisture-retardant chemical. If you buy treated lumber, make *sure* the chemicals are not toxic. Especially avoid pentachlorophenol, known as "penta." And don't use old railroad ties, which have been treated with creosote; it's harmful to plants. To be safe, use cedar or redwood, which naturally resist water damage.

An exciting new alternative is plastic lumber, made from a mixture of recycled wood and ground-up soda pop bottles. You can saw it, drill it, nail it just like wood, but it's weatherproof and a noteworthy example of recycling technology.

184 **A combination of raised beds and open garden works well.** If you have quite limited space, raised beds allow you to grow vegetables intensively. But if you are not restricted, you may be happier with a combination system. Think of it in terms of seasons: Save the open garden for summertime vegetables like corn, squash, cucumbers, and indeterminate tomatoes, which tend to take up lots of room. Use the raised beds—they're warmer, remember—for spring and fall crops.

Cool-season vegetables like peas, spinach, lettuce, broccoli, Brussels sprouts, and the like can go into the raised bed in February, March, and April. Then after they are harvested, pull out all the leftover plants, work in a new layer of compost, and you're ready to plant for fall: beets, carrots, turnips, more spinach, Swiss chard and oriental greens, and all the cabbage family.

Because you can start everything earlier with raised beds, you get can reliably get two full crops from the same space, and extend your growing season by several weeks on both ends—even more if you add floating row covers or plastic mulch.

Getting the Most from Your Space

◇185◇ **Grow as much as you can vertically.** Vining forms of squash and cucumbers, left to sprawl on the ground, consume enormous amounts of space. If you grow them upward, you get the same amount of produce, and maybe more, from a few square feet of ground space.

If your garden area is fenced in, use the fence as a growing area. If it's a chain-link fence, vining plants with tendrils will cling to it easily without any help from you. If it's a wooden fence, you'll probably want to add something for plants to grab onto. Cover the fence with chicken wire, or put a line of small nails or screw-eyes at top and bottom and run string between them. Or have a supply of twine nearby to tie the growing plants to the fence pickets. A length of the plastic mesh that is intended as a gutter screen, nailed to a fence post, makes a narrow trellis perfect for one cucumber vine.

If you don't have a fence, think about putting in a trellis, either temporary or permanent. The ready-made trellises sold in garden centers can be moved from place to place each season, but often they are comparatively flimsy; use them for lighter plants like peas, not heavy squash producers. If you have raised beds with wooden frames, attach several uprights to one of the end pieces (whichever one will not throw shadows on the garden), or to both ends and run a high crosspiece down the entire length of the bed.

No trellis or fence? Grow pole beans in the old-fashioned way. Stand three tall poles in the ground in a 3-foot triangle, then lash the tops together into a tepee shape. Plant several bean seeds next to each pole, and they'll wind their way up, filling in the walls of the tepee. Kids think this is terrific. If you have been pruning trees on your property, you may end up with long clear branches you can use for poles. If not, garden centers sell tall stakes—wood, metal, or bamboo—that work fine.

◈ **186** **Short portable supports can supplement or substitute for fences.** If you can't grow vines straight up, you can still get more out of your space by providing a short support that allows them to grow up one side and down the other. Build two stout frames about 4 feet square and hinge them together at the top; add nails or screw eyes for string or wire, or cover completely with chicken wire. Stand the frames open in the garden and plant a cucumber or squash along one side. When the season is over, fold them up and store.

Even easier alternative: use two wood pallets (warehouses often give away slightly damaged ones). Push the bottoms down into the soil and lean the tops together until they form a rigid A-frame.

Another way to go is short sections of wire fencing material or reinforcing wire, pushed into the ground far enough that they stand up on their own. Shape them into a Z or S layout for greater rigidity and space efficiency; plant your seeds in the notches of the Z.

Still another approach: flat panels made of four equal lengths of bamboo, lashed together at the four corners and strung vertically with twine. Leave a few inches bare on two bottom legs to push into the ground. Bamboo is lightweight but very strong.

‹187› Grow bush peas outside your tomato cages. If you make your own tomato cages from heavy wire with a wide grid (concrete-reinforcing wire, for instance) you can make much wider and stronger cages than the usual commercial cone-shaped product. And if you put them in the garden early in the spring, you can plant bush peas around the outside; they do better with a little support. Leave a door opening large enough to reach inside and plant your baby tomato in mid-May. The peas will be finished and ready to be pulled out about the same time the tomato is ready for a growth spurt.

188 **Move outside the main garden area to find pea and bean supports.** Walk around the southern side of your house or garage. Can you find a place where you could put in peas or beans alongside the wall and run supporting strings up to the house? One side of the front porch, maybe? The vines are attractive and make a wonderful living screen.

189 **Don't forget to look for space among the flower beds.** When you have deciduous perennials, there is a span of time in the spring when those plants haven't come up or are still very small. Use that space for early-spring crops. Many are attractive enough to stay in the flower bed all year long; you won't find a handsomer foliage plant than red-stemmed Swiss chard.

190 **Plant corn and winter squash together.** Something about the corn plant confuses squash vine beetles, and so you're likely to have less damage from them. Then, once the ears of corn have been harvested, train the squash vines to grow up the tall stalks. You can use sunflowers the same way, with summer squash.

◆ **191** **Plant near—or in—your compost bin.** Have you ever noticed how vigorously "volunteers" grow out the sides of your compost bin or pile? Take advantage of this rich concentrate of nutrients by deliberately planting along the edge. As microorganisms break down the organic material, nitrogen is leached out in the process. If you plant nitrogen-hungry crops nearby, like cucumbers or any of the leafy vegetables, they'll be able to use this important nutrient that would otherwise be lost. If you add garden soil to the top of the pile, which is good compost management anyway, you can plant right in the soil. Another advantage: you don't have to bend over so much.

◆ **192** **Plant thickly and interplant intensively.** If you plan carefully, you can squeeze quick-maturing plants in tightly among slower growers, and use up every inch of your growing space.

In very damp climates, this can be a tricky balancing act, for you also want to provide ample air circulation to prevent fungal diseases. One way to accommodate this balance is to plant thickly in the beginning and then thin the plants as they grow and begin to crowd each other. Many of these thinnings are tasty at that small size: spinach, lettuce, carrots, beets, for instance.

If your climate cooperates, there's a lot to be said for planting intensively. The less open ground there is between plants, the less room for weeds. You get more efficient use of water and fertilizer. If they are close together, plants like peppers, bush peas, bush beans will hold each other up and provide some protection against wind.

Even if moist conditions won't allow you to plant things very close together, you can still take advantage of succession planting. Think in terms of seasons: In the same space, start with early spring peas, then lettuce for late spring, then bush beans, then broccoli for fall and Swiss chard for winter. Any piece of bare soil should be your signal: what can I plant there right now?

193 **Grow cool-season plants in the shade of sun-lovers.** When your pole beans have filled out well with leaves, plant some lettuce or spinach inside the tepee. Or plant them underneath the collapsible A-frame trellises you've set up for cucumbers (see tip 186). If you grow vining cucumbers or squashes on a fence or trellis and can orient them so that their shade falls on part of the garden (or if you have no choice but to do so), use that shade for plants that tend to bolt in the hot sun, like broccoli, cabbage, or lettuce. This is not as perfect as spring planting, when the air as well as the soil is cool, but it's better than being in full sun.

Good Habits

194 **Watch the weather forecast closely.** In much of the Northwest, during much of the growing season, the weather can change dramatically from one day to the next. In May and June, and again in September and October, midday temperatures can vary as much as 20 degrees in a 24-hour period. Get in the habit of tuning in the evening weather forecast, and keep your cold-weather protection on standby.

195 **Keep a garden notebook.** And keep a separate record for each year. With a very few exceptions, vegetables are annuals. It is useful to track results over a period of several years, but the weather is such a wild card that any multi-year journal has to take that into account. It doesn't do you much good to note that a certain variety of lettuce flourished in 1995 if the 1996 spring season turns out to be much, much warmer. You'll get more solid information if you can compare variables during the same year: two different varieties of bush beans, planted at the same time; or the same type of cucumber in two different spots.

One of the easiest and best systems is to use one of those month-by-month calendars with an open square for each day and room to write in. Keep it near the door that's closest to the garden, along with a pencil. It takes only a minute to write down what you planted when, when you picked the first beans, when significant or surprising weather changes occurred, and so forth. And don't forget to note which things you liked the taste of.

◆196◆ Buy extras of hand tools, and keep them at handy locations.

When you find weeders, trowels, clippers, and so forth on sale at good prices, pick up some extras. Stash them at several work stations throughout the garden. Or keep one set by the front door and one by the back door. Or pick up an inexpensive mailbox and nail it to a garden fence post; store a working set here. These hand tools often show up at yard sales.

197 Save your old panty hose. They come in handy in several ways in the garden. Cut them into narrow strips to tie plant stems to stakes; they're very stretchy and, unlike wire-cored twist-ties, won't cut into tender stems. Use larger swatches as slings for large melons and squashes growing on vines up a fence; otherwise these heavy fruits could pull the vine down. Keep them intact to store cured bulb onions. Drop one down into the foot, tie a knot and drop another down, tie another knot, and so on. Hang the whole thing in the basement or utility room. When you need an onion, cut a segment from the bottom, and cut the snipped-off nylon into more narrow strips for next year.

198 Whenever you prune trees or shrubs, visualize using the prunings in the vegetable garden. Deciduous branches with lots of bare twigs make good support for peas. Thick limbs stripped of leaves can be bean poles or stout stakes for tomatoes. A cutting with lots of leaves can shade vulnerable seedlings during unseasonably hot days. Then onto the compost pile.

199 Plant a row for the hungry. I'm sure you already share the bounty of your vegetable garden with friends and neighbors; it's one of a gardener's great pleasures. This tip is about a more deliberate, planned action, and it is a movement gathering steam all around the country. When you plan your garden, set aside a row or more for the express purpose of donating its produce to a worthy cause in your area. This could be a homeless shelter, a community food bank, the local Meals on Wheels program, a church kitchen that prepares noon meals for seniors, whatever. While your special row is growing, use the time to research appropriate agencies in your area; find out what they can and cannot use, their preferred delivery times, and so on. It's not a good idea just to show up somewhere and dump off your extra tomatoes.

◇200◇ **Appreciate the magic.** While you're fighting the slugs, fretting over what's eating holes in your cabbage, or trying to remember how far apart to space corn seed, it's easy to get buried in the details and forget what this is all about. Why, after all, are you growing vegetables, when you could buy your food in the supermarket and avoid all these problems? Because of the wondrous fresh taste, and the enormous satisfaction of watching things grow.

Next time you're griping about how much work it all is, think about this: One little tomato seed, no bigger than the head of a pin, will grow into a full-size plant, loaded with enough tomatoes to make a whole summer's worth of salads, plus many to share with others. Every vegetable plant is a small, self-contained miracle, and it's happening right in front of our eyes.

APPENDIX: MORE INFORMATION, GOOD SOURCES

❧ ❧ ❧

Seed Catalogs

Abundant Life Seed Foundation, PO Box 772, Port Townsend, WA 98368. 360-385-5660. Catalog free; $2 donation appreciated.

Nonprofit organization dedicated to enhancing genetic diversity and preserving native, heirloom, and endangered seeds. Most of the seeds they sell were trialed in Washington state and were chosen because they do well in the Northwest.

The Cook's Garden, PO Box 535, Londonderry, VT 05148, 802-824-3400. Catalog $1.

A small, family-run company with a strong environmental focus, from a long line of organic gardeners. Catalog features their specialty—a wide selection of lettuces and other salad greens—and Ellen Ogden's recipes.

Deep Diversity Seeds of Change, PO Box 15189, Santa Fe, NM 87596-5189. Catalog free.

Most of the vegetable seeds offered from this alternative company were produced in Oregon (identified as such in the catalog) and should do well in all areas of the maritime Northwest.

Harris Seeds, 60 Saginaw Drive, PO Box 22960, Rochester, NY 14692-2960. 716-442-0410. Catalog free.

A general-purpose collection from a company in business more than 100 years. Varieties are chosen for the Northeast, with climate conditions similar to the maritime Northwest.

Ed Hume Seeds, PO Box 1450, Kent, WA 98034. Catalog $1.

From the popular teacher and TV personality, a good selection of the basics, chosen with Northwest growing conditions in mind.

Le Jardin du Gourmet, PO Box 75, St. Johnsbury Center, VT 05863. Catalog free.

Catalog contains no illustrations or cultural information, but if you already know what variety you want, this company offers something unique: small sample packets of seeds for 25 cents each. Imports from France many seeds of gourmet vegetables.

Johnny's Selected Seeds, Foss Hill Rd, Albion, ME 04910. 207-437-9294. Catalog free.

An impressive selection of vegetables, both standard and unusual, presented with thorough growing information. Company produces many of its own seeds; maturity dates on packets reflect Maine environment, with cool summers—like the Northwest. Catalog uses symbols to designate varieties that tolerate cool weather, do well in containers, etc.

Nichols Garden Nursery, 1190 N. Pacific Highway, Albany, OR 97321, 503-928-9280. Catalog free.

Now in its 46th year, Nichols has an all-purpose selection of vegetables and many varieties of everything. The catalog uses a special symbol to designate varieties that do especially well in the Northwest.

Redwood City Seed Co, PO Box 361, Redwood City, CA 94064. 415-325-7333. Catalog $1.

The original "alternative" seed company; their goal is preservation of endangered cultivated plants. Catalog features both traditional and unusual vegetables, all chosen for a short-season maritime climate.

Ronnigers, Star Rt, Moyie Springs, ID 83845. Catalog $2.

Organically grown seed potatoes—just what you'd expect from a company located in Idaho.

Seeds Trust Inc, PO Box 1048, Hailey, ID 83333-2048. 208-788-4363. Catalog $3.

Part of this company's name is High-Altitude Gardens. All the varieties are chosen for high-atitude, short-season areas, and the first piece of information given for each vegetable is its frost tolerance. Strong organic focus, nice selection of vegetables, and casy-to-read catalog.

Shepherd's Garden Seeds, 6116 Highway 9, Felton, CA 95018. 408-335-6910. Catalog free.

A personal favorite. Renee Shepherd has stuffed her catalog with vegetables chosen because they taste good; many are imported from Europe, including gourmet varieties not available elsewhere. Extremely thorough descriptions of each variety, including cooking ideas, and cogent gardening information.

Territorial Seed Company, PO Box 157, Cottage Grove, OR 97424. 503-942-9547. Catalog free.

Produces a special catalog for the Northwest, with varieties chosen for areas west of the Cascades. Includes complete gardening information and symbols designating varieties that do well in cool areas, containers, winter gardens, etc.

National seed companies

All-purpose companies with wide selections of vegetables; catalogs are free.

Burpee & Co., Warminster, PA 18974

Gurney's Seed & Nursery, 110 Capital St., Yankton, SD 57079

Park Seed, Cokesbury Rd, Greenwood, SC 29647-0001

County Extension Offices/Master Gardeners

State agricultural colleges are, through their extensive research programs, the original source of many of the vegetables we now grow in home gardens. Dr. James Baggett at Oregon State University is mentioned several times in this book; others have made comparable contributions, but I'm an Oregonian and therefore partial. These state universities are also a rich source of information for home gardeners, primarily through field offices in each county, known as County Extension Offices. These extension offices operate a little differently in each state, but all provide information geared to the specific growing conditions of the area.

Look in the government pages of your local phone book, under the name of your county; the office is usually listed as Extension Service or Cooperative Extension Service. The staff person you want may have the title of Extension Agent, Home Horticulture Specialist, or Urban Horticulturist. Take the time to find the office in your county; the wealth of information they have will amaze you, and it's all free.

If you are unable to locate your county office, or if there isn't one where you live, contact the statewide office and ask for the closest extension office:

Idaho
    Cooperative Extension Service
    Agricultural College
    University of Idaho
    Moscow, ID 83843

Montana
    Cooperative Extension Service
    Montana State University
    901 N. Black
    Bozeman, MT 59715

Oregon

Cooperative Extension Service
School of Agriculture
Oregon State University
Corvallis, OR 97331-4202

Washington

Cooperative Extension Service
Washington State University
Pullman, WA 99146-5912

California has no one statewide office; check with the Agriculture Department at the branch of the University of California that is closest to you.

The Master Gardener program, usually housed in the same location as the county extension office and often run by the same people, provides free training in gardening skills in exchange for volunteer service. When you call your local extension office with specific questions, often your call will be handled by a Master Gardener. Local Master Gardener programs also hold special seminars and fairs, with lots of knowledgeable people around.

Statewide Master Gardener Coordinators

Oregon Ray McNeilan, extension agent for Multnomah, Clackamas, and Washington counties, 503-254-1500.

Washington Van Bobbitt, urban horticulturist, Puyallup, 206-840-4500.

Idaho Dr. Michael Colt, extension horticulturist, University of Idaho, 208-722-6701; Kevin Laughlin, Sand Point, 208-263-8511.

Montana Helen Atthowe, home horticulture specialist, Missoula, 406-721-4095.

California Does not have a statewide coordinator; individual counties may have Master Gardener programs, as funding permits. County Extension Office personnel usually available to answer questions.

Farmers' Markets

Throughout the Northwest, many communities have farmers' markets, where local growers bring in produce to one central site. It's a wonderful source for fresh vegetables and fruits—and for invaluable information. Usually the sellers are also the growers, and so you can talk to them about the varieties they've had best success with. Often they sell vegetable seedlings too. These are experienced gardeners who live very near you; take advantage of what they have learned.

INDEX

❦ ❦ ❦

Please note: the numbers below refer to the tips, not the book's pages.